Praise for *Wellbeing Intelligence*

"*Wellbeing Intelligence* is the book we all need to develop mental health self-care. It is full of practical, timely and science-based advice to foster healthier careers and organisations."

Dorie Clark, *Wall Street Journal* bestselling author of *The Long Game* and executive education faculty, Columbia Business School

"We all know wellbeing is the major issue of the times. Yet we don't know what to do about it. In this immensely practical, beyond-the-hype book you have the guide you need to sustainably improve your own, your employees' and your organisation's wellbeing."

Herminia Ibarra, Charles Handy Professor of Organisational Behaviour, London Business School

"*Wellbeing Intelligence* is that rare thing: a practical but also incredibly clear and well-written book for individuals and managers in any workplace. At a time when burnout and workplace absence through mental health issues is a global problem, the authors have distilled clear action plans and better self-awareness – for ourselves and for our colleagues and teams. It deserves to be on every team leader's (and member's) bookshelf."

Isabel Berwick, "Working It" editor, *Financial Times*

"In *Wellbeing Intelligence*, Bhatti and Roulet offer a critical perspective on managing mental health at work. This book is an essential tool for anyone aiming to navigate the complexities of modern work environments with resilience and intentionality."

Hector D. Mujica, Head of Americas Philanthropy, Google.org

Wellbeing Intelligence

Wellbeing Intelligence

Building better mental health at work

Kiran Bhatti and Thomas Roulet

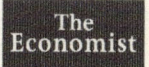

Published in 2025 under exclusive licence from The Economist by
Profile Books Ltd
29 Cloth Fair
London EC1A 7JQ
www.profilebooks.com

We make every effort to make sure our products are safe for the purpose for which
they are intended. For more information check our website or contact Authorised Rep
Compliance Ltd., Ground Floor, 71 Lower Baggot Street, Dublin, D02 P593, Ireland,
www.arccompliance.com

ISBN 978 1 80081 973 3
eISBN 978 1 80081 974 0

Typeset in Economist Serif by MacGuru Ltd
Printed and bound in India by Manipal Technologies Limited, Manipal

MIX
Paper | Supporting
responsible forestry
FSC™ C104740

About the authors

Kiran Bhatti is a chartered counselling psychologist. She obtained her PhD at the University of Roehampton, where her research focused on psychometrics. She has many years of experience providing therapeutic support to a range of individuals and groups across the NHS, third sector and education settings. In addition to her clinical practice, Kiran writes and researches on employee wellbeing, workplace stress and mental health, and has published in the *MIT Sloan Management Review*, *Harvard Business Review* and research journals in counselling psychology.

Thomas Roulet is the Professor of Organisational Sociology and Leadership at the Cambridge Judge Business School, and a Fellow in Psychology and Behavioural Science at King's College, University of Cambridge. His work focuses on stigma, the future of work, mental health in the workplace and communication. His comments are featured regularly in the *Financial Times*, *The Economist*, Bloomberg, the *Telegraph* and *Le Monde* and on the BBC. In 2024, he was recognised as one of the Young Global Leaders by the World Economic Forum, and as an upcoming leadership thinker by Thinkers50, MT/Sprout and Nexxworks. He was made a Mid-Career Fellow of the British Academy in 2023. In 2020, he was listed among the "40 under 40 best business school professors" by Poets & Quants, and as a "business school professor to look for" by Business Because. He has taken his research and learning to dozens of firms and public organisations as a speaker and consultant and through the design of executive education programmes.

Also in the Economist Edge series

Branding That Means Business
Matt Johnson and Tessa Misiaszek

Innovating with Impact
Ted Ladd and Alessandro Lanteri

Giving Good Feedback
Margaret Cheng

Best Story Wins: Storytelling for business success
Mark Edwards

Influence at Work
Steve Martin

The Power of Culture: Bringing values to life at work
Laura Hamill

Choose Trust: Building relationships for business success
Stuart Maister and Kevin Vaughan-Smith

For our clients, colleagues and students who inspired us to develop the concept of wellbeing intelligence and share it at work and beyond.

Contents

Introduction

The last few years have been intense, from pandemics to political and economic instability, and no organisation has been spared. Yours is no exception. Staff turnover may have gone through the roof, and recruiting the right people – and motivating them – has become increasingly difficult. You've become used to cycles of quiet quitting, great resignations and roaring waves of recruitment.

Just today, you have a new resignation letter on your desk. Another person in your team has decided to leave: the work pressure, the stress has got the better of them. It seems like this is affecting not only those who joined in the last few years – who sometimes failed to connect with the organisation and their teammates – but also the people who have been working for the company for five years or more. You have been feeling quite demotivated yourself. Coming to work has become harder. It does not make much sense any more.

Sound familiar? It has been for many people at work. Although wellbeing issues in the workplace are not new, they have been reinforced by the changes the workplace has experienced in the last few years. These changes will only accelerate, and it's hard to say whether they will all be positive. When the home-based workforce doubled with the shift to remote work caused by national lockdowns in 2020, many looked at this sudden shift with rose-tinted glasses; and plenty of organisations reported a peak in productivity.[1]

But the loss of boundaries between work and life also had negative implications for mental health, with employees struggling to disconnect. The burnout epidemic spread like wildfire as some workers were laid off or furloughed, leaving fewer people behind to manage a reeling boat in the middle of the most significant storm of the century. In March 2020, according to Gallup, the percentage of US adults who reported experiencing worry during their workday suddenly jumped by 20 points, from 38% to 58%.

Add to this a more general sense of uncertainty about the future – everything from the climate crisis to the dangers of artificial intelligence – and it's little wonder that our awareness of mental health challenges in organisations has been heightened. These have become so acute that they can no longer be ignored. Managers, employees and human resource teams are faced with a wave of burnout, a rise in anxiety levels and depression. And this tsunami has organisational implications that require shifts in mindsets and culture. Almost half of the workforce report experiencing stress – the highest it has ever been.[2] Yet surveys show that the support for employee wellbeing has declined since 2021 among senior leaders.[3]

On its own, awareness of mental health issues in the workplace isn't enough to deal with one of the biggest challenges faced by organisations today: the preservation and nurturing of their people. Research also shows that, in our understanding of work, the drivers of wellbeing vary from one person to the other. Therefore blanket approaches are unlikely to work. Instead, individuals need to improve their understanding of their own wellbeing and the wellbeing of others. In a nutshell, wellbeing skills need to be democratised in the workplace and available to everyone.

Currently, the way we learn and develop these skills takes

either a single-minded psychological approach or a gimmicky and unsatisfying managerial approach. There have been many articles in management journals and books on mental health in the workplace in the last few years. They tend either to take a solely clinical approach on what mental health is all about or, conversely, they approach it narrowly by looking at how it affects the bottom line of organisations, talking in generalities rather than taking into account the people who have to deal with mental health challenges on a daily basis. They are descriptive. Similarly, psychology research has also given a prominent space to mental health and relevant interventions in organisations, but without necessarily considering the practical implications for people on the ground.

For a long time, mental health remained a rather abstract and elusive concept for most people at work. They might have perceived it as a potential threat to their team and organisation but were unclear about what that might mean in practice.

Because of the sudden new visibility of the issue, many have started to put a name on some of the challenges they experience. And they are also increasingly more likely to see it first hand, playing out in front of their eyes. But people are often clueless about how to tackle those issues, whether on an organisational level or simply how to talk to colleagues who are experiencing mental health challenges. What would be the right words? The right tone? The right attitude and approach? How can they improve and refine their approach to wellbeing?

So people know that mental health challenges exist, but they do not know how to address and approach them. Insight might sharpen sensitivity to challenges, but unpacking the complexities of dealing with them is missing. What's needed is a more prescriptive approach that answers two key questions. How can you concretely improve and address mental wellbeing at work? And how can everyone in organisations develop wellbeing skills over time and with experience?

The aim of this book is to pass on practical skills that focus on understanding and addressing mental health in the workplace. People need more than self-help mental health books or basic diagnoses that mental health issues in organisations are rife. They already know that. Mental health skills need to be a well-defined area of organisational and individual development. This book offers the keys to develop these skills.

A new perspective

To explore those questions, we want to make use of the wisdom of mental health practitioners who have worked for decades to support people within and outside the workplace. Their skills are derived from models and techniques that have empirically proven effective. We want to bring the topics of organisational management and mental health together, building on our expertise as a psychologist and management professor respectively.

Interdisciplinarity is often presented as the paragon of good academic research. Yet we thought of our respective careers as silos for the first years of our relationship. (Beyond writing a book together, we are also married to each other.) We quickly realised the synergies in our skills and the wide appetite for such a multidisciplinary perspective: Kiran bringing the technical expertise and proven methods of psychologists to improve wellbeing, and Thomas the organisational and managerial viewpoint.

Like many, and probably like most of the readers of this book, we have struggled with our wellbeing at work and in our personal lives, from anxiety and stress to depression. Experiencing those struggles first hand has pushed us to read, explore and practise so that we can understand and help ourselves better (and each other). The principles we found have guided our own careers and we have also passed on what we have learnt to clients and students alike.

Now we want to share what we've learnt and practised more widely. This is the book we wished we had had when we wanted to support ourselves and others in our organisations. It offers a toolkit that is versatile but effective, based on approaches and methods that everybody can learn, apply and refine to improve their own – and others' – wellbeing at work.

Who is this book for?

The answer is simple: everybody who has a keen interest in understanding their own wellbeing and the wellbeing of others and wants to act to improve it. Understanding mental health in its full complexity, its sources and outcomes, is not an add-on for organisations; it is a must-have. Through our wellbeing intelligence (WBQ) model, we want to encourage people not just to be sensitive to wellbeing issues and challenges at work, but also to adapt their behaviour and take action. The book offers a "first aid kit" for wellbeing that will help you to understand your own mental health and to identify colleagues in difficult situations who need support.

This book is not just for "managers" or "leaders" with positional and organisational authority; it's for anyone navigating any workplace.

Workplace stress does not differentiate between different sectors and contexts and neither does the book. It does not differentiate between age groups, or individual experience. The book is relevant for people working at the biggest corporations or the smallest business; for police officers, teachers and healthcare workers; for not-for-profit and government organisations.

That's not to say that senior leaders don't have a crucial role to play; top executives set the tone and the culture for their organisations and can give visibility to mental health issues by sharing their own experiences. For example, Winston Churchill experienced depression before the First World War and shared how creative activities helped him address this challenge.[4] The behaviours of top executives can have a huge cultural impact, helping to normalise discussions about mental health and making mental health challenges more likely to be detected and addressed. We exhort leaders to be mental health advocates. But to do so, they first need to understand what that means.

We are not, of course, suggesting that benefiting from the practical knowledge of psychology will make you all psychologists. Counselling psychologists have often received years of training, practised with multiple types of patients and conditions, and developed unique skills to support others. In many cases, you simply won't be able to fully address people's mental health issues; they will need professional help. But you can still provide support and understanding. By building up your knowledge of mental health and your wellbeing intelligence, you will be able to provide some genuine relief without the risk of making things worse.

A holistic perspective on wellbeing

Our perspective on wellbeing is holistic, but with a distinct focus on mental health. The *Cambridge Dictionary* defines wellbeing as "the state of being healthy and happy". We recognise that wellbeing can include both physical and mental health, but also believe that both aspects overlap and are difficult to distinguish: 46% of people with a mental health issue in England, for example, have a long-term physical condition.[5] In this book, we'll focus on the mental health aspect of wellbeing, while considering physical and mental health to be interdependent. And although there are hundreds of books on the best diet, the best exercise routine and how you can take care of your body, practical routines to strengthen mental health are surprisingly missing from existing models of wellbeing. This book aims to fill that gap.

How to use this book

This book unfolds over ten chapters in four parts.

Part 1 explores the present state of wellbeing, and the short- and long-term mental health challenges faced by organisations today. It defines the key mental health phenomena in organisations so that you are aware of the definitions attached to sometimes abstract ideas such as anxiety or depression, and other associated issues. And it introduces our concentric circle model of wellbeing intelligence as a road map for better wellbeing at work.

Parts 2–4 look at the three circles of wellbeing intelligence.

This starts with a focus on the self – helping you to understand your own wellbeing. Self-awareness is also a major first step to understanding the mental health of others. Part 2 provides a clear and actionable approach to your own mental health and distils several self-assessment tools and frameworks commonly used in counselling.

Part 3 looks at the group level. What should leaders and team members know about mental health when working together and in one-to-one relationships? What can they do to detect issues and to support each other?

Part 4 explores approaches, policies and strategies to improve mental health and wellbeing at an organisational level.

In sum, what follows is a toolkit that offers practical models, frameworks and assessment tools to help everyone to be not only wellbeing aware but also wellbeing intelligent.

PART 1

Why do we need wellbeing intelligence?

PART I

Why do we need wellbeing intelligence?

Estephania had been in disarray for the past few weeks. She had never experienced such a difficult situation in her ten years as commercial director at Software Inc. Yes, sales had been at their lowest for a while, but Software Inc was still in good shape despite the global recession. Yet the sales team she managed had become impossible. She did not even know where to start. Members were disengaged, and had lost enthusiasm for their work, the company or the products. Conflicts between team members had become rampant.

She had tried everything from the carrot to the stick: encouraging those who were making more effort and scaring others by telling them the consequences of their disengagement. It was time to explore a new course of action and a new method. She had thought that this situation was due to a problem of management or uncertainty about the future of the company, but she had started to realise this was probably only a small part of the story. To add to her confusion, she herself was struggling with a difficult situation at home, which made her more irritable at work.

Estephania's instincts are right. She needs to think beyond classic management tools. The problem is not a managerial one; it is about wellbeing. Her people are mentally and emotionally exhausted, and their frustration with management is only the symptom of an issue that has spread in the team. Like many other people at work right now, Estephania needs wellbeing intelligence (WBQ).

Part 1 introduces the topic of wellbeing in the workplace from the dual perspective of management research and counselling psychology. What is wellbeing? What are core wellbeing issues, and how can we identify and define them? The objective is to demystify things like stress, anxiety and other mental health struggles. Those who have experienced them know why they matter and why we should care both individually and collectively. But wellbeing also needs to become a key priority for everyone at work, whether they are affected personally or not.

We spend a significant part of our life at work, and the boundaries between work and home life are more blurred than ever. What happens at work can have life-changing consequences. This first section of the book focuses on raising awareness of wellbeing issues and shaping our understanding of how they evolve and manifest themselves.

1

Wellbeing at work and why it matters

Let's start by laying the foundations for wellbeing intelligence: clear definitions, a rationale for learning about wellbeing, and the conditions under which you can develop it

If you were to ask Estephania to consider the wellbeing of her team members and her own wellbeing, she might well ask: what does that mean? The word is commonly used but nobody seems to be able to offer a robust or consistent definition. It's often associated with people meditating in front of a sunset, or smiling and laughing in a social setting. Such caricatures do not mean we should overthink it. Wellbeing can simply be defined as feeling good about yourself, the world around you, and life in general. It refers to overall good quality of life. Given how much of our life we spend at work, wellbeing at work clearly matters.

American psychologist Margaret (Peggy) Swarbrick has identified eight dimensions of wellbeing, as outlined in Figure 1 on the next page. For Swarbrick, people's levels of wellbeing can fluctuate depending on a range of factors. For example, financial wellbeing, which relates to earning potential or savings, might vary according to the cost of living or other economic factors; if we suddenly have to take a pay cut, we may feel less financially well. This might negatively affect our overall wellbeing, even

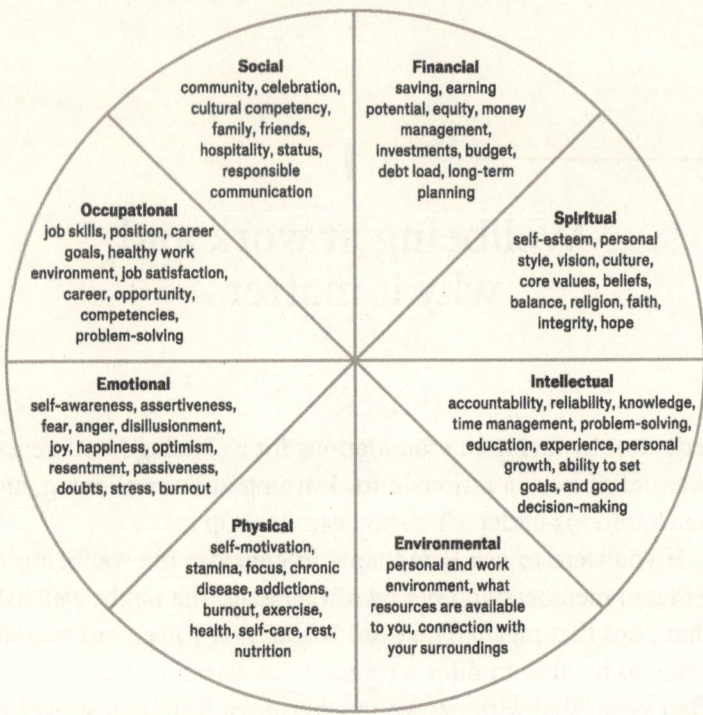

Social
community, celebration, cultural competency, family, friends, hospitality, status, responsible communication

Financial
saving, earning potential, equity, money management, investments, budget, debt load, long-term planning

Occupational
job skills, position, career goals, healthy work environment, job satisfaction, career, opportunity, competencies, problem-solving

Spiritual
self-esteem, personal style, vision, culture, core values, beliefs, balance, religion, faith, integrity, hope

Emotional
self-awareness, assertiveness, fear, anger, disillusionment, joy, happiness, optimism, resentment, passiveness, doubts, stress, burnout

Intellectual
accountability, reliability, knowledge, time management, problem-solving, education, experience, personal growth, ability to set goals, and good decision-making

Physical
self-motivation, stamina, focus, chronic disease, addictions, burnout, exercise, health, self-care, rest, nutrition

Environmental
personal and work environment, what resources are available to you, connection with your surroundings

Figure 1: **Swarbrick's eight dimensions of wellbeing**[1]

if we're experiencing high wellbeing in other areas of our life. Although there are many aspects to wellbeing, each aspect will feed into each other and into our overall quality of life. We may just have completed our first half marathon, but that sudden pay cut will still have an impact.

Although this book has a specific focus on what Swarbrick calls "occupational wellbeing", we will not treat occupational wellbeing in isolation. If you think about it, wellbeing at work is not *just* about those occupational factors. It also needs to factor in our financial and intellectual wellbeing; take into account the interconnectedness of our physical and mental health; and consider the environmental, spiritual and social spheres that contribute to and set the scene for how we feel. Wellbeing at work is about wellbeing in the round.

This perspective on wellbeing also leads to a focus on a central pillar and enabler of our wellbeing: our mental health. Without mental health, wellbeing in its multiple dimensions is only a distant possibility. Across the world, there are people with mental health issues, though the awareness of such issues varies between cultures and institutions. According to the World Health Organisation, mental distress and depression is the leading cause of disability worldwide.[2] The term "disability" in itself signals that mental health can be a factor of exclusion in society and in organisations. It is estimated that 4.4% of the global population live with depression, and 3.6% of the global population are affected by anxiety disorders.[3]

If geographical or cultural barriers are not stopping mental health issues, the barrier between people's professional and personal lives is just as porous. Estimates suggest that people spend, on average, up to 90,000 hours at work in their lives – leaving aside the extra hours worked beyond contractual minimums, household and caring tasks or the people who work multiple jobs. Wherever you work and whatever the specific make-up of your career, you spend a significant proportion of your life working and at work. It's bound to have an impact on your mental health and wellbeing.

Work can mean a lot of things to us individually and collectively. Yes, it is a paycheque; it provides a wage and is a way to make a living. But work can be so much more: the chance to make an impact, a sense of achievement, a source of pride and a way to build lasting connections with others. A review of the scientific literature on the relationship between life satisfaction and the work domain establishes a clear link between work satisfaction, feelings of self-worth and, ultimately, life satisfaction.[4] When people enjoy work, they feel better about themselves, and they enjoy life as well. That makes sense: work can be a great source of joy and self-esteem. In turn, increased life satisfaction limits people's negative feelings towards their work. When people enjoy life, they tend to have a more positive outlook on work too.

The opposite is also true, and bad experiences at work can turn into a vicious rather than a virtuous cycle of wellbeing. Poor satisfaction at work can have a negative effect on feelings of self-worth and life satisfaction. When people feel miserable at work, they tend to lose confidence and life gets bleak. There are many workplace factors that drive mental health difficulties. Being constantly assessed and judged; being put under consistent pressure; cultures of competition or aggressive leadership styles: all can have an impact on people's mental health and lead to high levels of stress. Work can make people unhappy, and not only at work.

In a nutshell, work and mental health are strongly interconnected: poor mental health at work can spread outside work and exacerbate life difficulties, and personal difficulties can spill over into the work environment. Social scientists call this a "work–life spillover". People often make sense of life through work, and find solace and purpose in it when the work they are doing is impactful. But when they are in distress, struggling to fulfil job roles and duties and unable to connect fully with colleagues, they may begin to avoid going into work, and start to disengage with other areas of life too.

Mental health issues should be a central preoccupation because they matter hugely for society and for people. They are "disabling" because they disconnect individuals from what can motivate them, fuel them and give them purpose in life and at work. People with mental health issues are unable to reach their full potential. Collectively, this makes the economic and social costs of mental health far-reaching.

Mental health and working cannot and should not be separated. Your mental health can influence how you work. Equally, your work environment can influence your mental health. Work can be both the cause of, and the solution to, feeling happier, engaged and well.

Mental health at work

Globally, one third of women and one fifth of men will experience depression over their lifetime.[5] It is estimated that 4% of people worldwide suffer from an anxiety disorder.[6] Within the UK, it is estimated one in six adults experience a common mental health difficulty (anxiety or depression) within any given week.[7] It's also estimated that about 15% of the workforce in England experiences symptoms of mental health problems at work.[8]

But the prevalence of mental health issues is not only about trends and numbers. Both professionally and personally, individual lives can be deeply affected. For example, it is estimated that each year 300,000 people with long-term mental health conditions lose their jobs.[9] And those figures do not include those with undiagnosed mental health problems, such as stress, burnout and worry. The numbers also do not include those people who have not disclosed their difficulties and who have not received a formal diagnosis. The real number of people suffering mental distress may be much greater than reported.

Even allowing for these factors, it's clear that the number of people experiencing and reporting mental health difficulties at work is increasing at a worrying rate. It's not surprising that organisations are increasingly aware that it's an important factor in whether people can contribute and succeed at work, and a crucial determinant of their performance.

The invisibility of mental health at work

Despite these concerning figures, wellbeing is not something that you can always "see" at work. Mental health issues can be invisible because they are often unspoken, especially in a world where many work interactions have shifted online. Yet, if you dig deeper, the experience aligns with the numbers: it would be hard to find an organisation where people have not experienced some degree of mental health challenge.

It's tempting to think that visible physical illness is more measurable and can be "seen". But, as Chapter 2 explores, there are a range of scientifically robust survey tools and more informal ways to identify the presence of mental health issues at individual, group and organisational levels. But people still need a fine-grained understanding of wellbeing issues, what causes them and how to describe them. Individuals might be experiencing a mix of anxiety, stress and depression, and the combination of those factors might not fall into one easily defined category.

Experiencing mental health problems can also be a source of stigmatisation and social exclusion. Not understanding mental health issues often means negating their existence. From the perspective of those who have not experienced them, mental health issues can sometimes be perceived as having no material basis or cause. Some people may be tempted to see mental health issues as an effort to grab attention, as a fake affliction that people can conquer by sheer willpower. As a result, people with mental health issues might experience less sympathy at work than those with visible physical health issues. Such beliefs often need to be addressed as the first thing an organisation can do to create a positive culture towards mental health and help make mental health issues more noticeable.

The only way for those problems to be visible is if people speak about them – particularly their own challenges. Enabling a work context where people are comfortable speaking about how they're feeling and trust that they won't be stigmatised as a result depends on the way mental health is perceived.

Talking about mental health can, however, be tricky. Because mental health is a primarily invisible and a potentially sensitive challenge, it's often hard to find the right way to approach it. The fear of doing things incorrectly, of saying something wrong, means that it can be tempting to say and do nothing. Consequently, mental health might remain unaddressed with all the problems accumulated both at an individual level (e.g. burnout and people having to take time off to recover) and at an organisational level (e.g. a culture of overwork from which people struggle to disconnect).

Existing research shows that those who receive emotional support for mental health from their colleagues are not always aware of it.[10] The simple act of listening might not feel like mental health support, but it can be especially effective because it does not feel like "treatment". This evidence also suggests that a deep understanding of mental health is needed to tackle issues with care and sensitivity. And deep understanding starts with clear definitions of the core labels.

The costs of poor mental health for organisations

Visible or invisible, there are many tangible consequences of poor mental health in the workplace. These can include poor team morale, loss of productivity, high employee turnover, disengagement with work, lower work quality, disidentification (when employees feel emotionally distant from their organisations) and many other negative outcomes. If left untreated or unacknowledged, mental health difficulties can develop into longer-term problems, meaning greater resources and investments are needed over time to help organisations cope with them.

On an individual level, poor mental health will obviously affect a person's experience within their organisation but, as we have seen, it is by no means isolated to their workplace. Physical health is also affected by the physiological consequences of poor mental health, including back, neck and shoulder pains, increased blood pressure, nausea and heart problems.[11] Evidence suggests that mood and anxiety disorders are associated with an increased risk of cardiovascular disease.[12] The behavioural consequences of workplace stress, such as poor diet and sleep, will also contribute to poor physical health.

The vicious cycle of mental and physical challenges can be aggravated by what are often called "self-medicating" behaviours or coping mechanisms. Those reactions can include smoking, substance use or alcohol use, ultimately worsening physical and mental health altogether. Substance abuse might "take the edge off" in the short term, but the backlash can be terrible. Recent research has even found that a poor day at work could increase potentially fatal risk-taking – like going through a red light on the drive home from work.[13]

As the boundaries between work and life have been eroded, our professional activities are often a very large share of how we perceive our lives in general. Workplace stressors are increasingly beginning to seep into the home environment and negatively affect family relationships and dynamics. For example, how many of you have had to carry out extra work over a weekend, meaning less time with your family, putting you in a bad mood and making you short-tempered? Work–life spillover and cumulative work stress can begin to undermine many of the benefits of family and partner relationships, as the sense of support and security from people close to you, typically used to overcome stressors, becomes threatened.

The devastating consequences that poor mental health can have for individuals and their relationship with work also has wider implications. Individuals experiencing poor mental health at work are likely to report greater levels of burnout and are less likely to remain in secure employment. Such instability has a compounding effect and creates a vicious cycle that progressively excludes them from the workforce, depriving organisations of their skills and expertise. And the vicious cycle lingers because unemployed people are more likely to experience worry, anxiety and depression, further preventing a healthy return to work. Being unable to work because of mental health reinforces anxiety and depression.

Figure 2 on the next page shows how poor mental health at work can create a vicious cycle in which mental distress and its consequences perpetuate poor mental health and affect both individuals and organisations. In contrast, when mentally healthy individuals are able to fully engage in their working lives, they benefit themselves, their team, their organisation and the wider community.

At an organisational level, poor mental health can be devastating. The link is clear: increased stress and other mental health challenges reduce motivation and productivity for workers, which in turn affects the organisation. As we have seen, it is also likely to increase staff turnover. Luckily, the converse is also true: positive satisfaction goes hand in hand with wellbeing at work and improves productivity, which reminds us that organisations have it in their power to turn those vicious cycles around.[14]

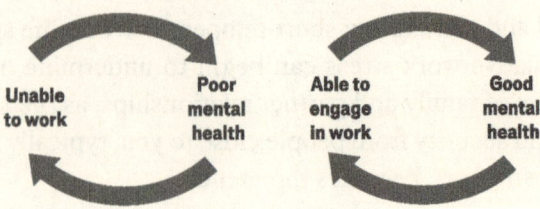

Figure 2: **Vicious and virtuous cycles of mental health at work**

The key to understanding how mental health affects organisations is to look at what social scientists call "mediating" mechanisms. Mental health affects a range of factors (such as individual performance, work motivation, engagement, citizenship behaviour and organisational climate), which themselves affect organisational performance. For example, an individual's poor mental health may have a rapid impact on a team's cohesiveness, as colleagues may have to take on additional work to meet organisational demands. In this sense, burnout may trigger yet more burnout as the load is passed on to others. Figure 3 shows this trickling-up effect from individuals to group and organisational levels.

An expert in Chinese antiques shared her story after leaving a prestigious art dealers. As her colleagues experienced burnout from increased workloads, she ended up taking on their work too, tackling tasks that were beyond the scope of her expertise, such as preparing the antiques for sales. This not only caused her own workload to grow, but also frustration at not being able to do her work correctly, and the feeling of being undervalued contributed to her own burnout.

The art dealers ended up losing key people in a specialised field in which expertise is narrow and rare. On top of that, clients were being turned away by the poor quality of service

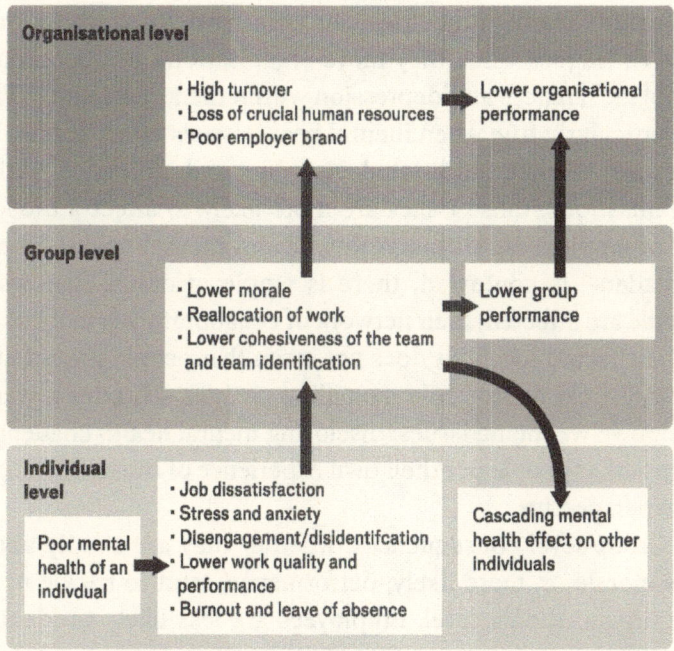

Figure 3: **Consequences of mental health issues at the individual, group and organisational levels**

from employees who were willing to do well but were not trained to carry out their tasks. This is a clear example of how the organisational context can lead to mental health issues, which then affect a range of other factors, ultimately damaging the bottom line. Inevitably, the firm's prestige and status (which were strong selling points) declined – and so did sales.

The risk of a domino effect is real: one individual's struggle can have widespread consequences on their team and their organisation. A controversial piece of research in 2022 explored the existence of this contagion effect of depression and anxiety by looking at how employees from organisations with high levels of mental health difficulties can even have an effect on their new colleagues when they move organisations and potentially "implant" anxiety and depression within their new team.[15] This is particularly true when mental health issues affect managers; because of their additional visibility and influence within organisations, those issues are more likely to affect a broader set of employees. Although this idea of mental health "super-spreaders" is contested, there is ample evidence that when people are affected, their network of collaborators is more likely to be affected too. This does not mean that people should hide their distress or stop role modelling positive attitudes towards their own wellbeing issues: disclosing mental health challenges helps other people put their own experience of those challenges into perspective.

Group-level consequences, whether they are simply about low morale or, more likely, performance, tend to trickle up to the organisational level. Employees are less likely to identify with their organisations (i.e. feel like their personal identity and self-perception overlap significantly with the identity and image of their organisation) when they are frustrated with their work. High levels of turnover will then turn into higher recruiting costs and a weaker employer brand or ability to attract the best talent. Mental health costs can occur on both sides of the equation, raising costs and lowering the value of the best employees. For example, experiencing high levels of stress and anxiety at work can result in both increased employee presenteeism (as employees compensate for what they feel is a mental health-related loss of productivity) and absenteeism (because mental health issues might ultimately force people into leave of absence).

Mental health in the workplace is an issue not only for organisations but also for society as a whole. Untreated problems can cause additional costs to health, social and educational services. It is estimated that poor mental health costs UK employers up to £45bn each year,[16] meaning that more money is lost from poor mental health at work than NHS funding for mental health services in the UK.[17]

And because individuals with mental health difficulties at work are less likely to remain in secure employment, they are more likely to receive welfare benefits.[18] The situation is made worse if efforts are not made to support people so they can get back into employment.

On every level, it is vital to invest in individuals' mental health at work. Organisations and leaders are in a prime position to contribute to this investment. When people thrive at work, their mental health benefits. This creates a healthy cycle in which both the individual and the organisation prosper. Organisations that lead on mental health can build up a stronger employer brand to attract more talented and diverse employees. They can limit turnover and retain, develop and motivate their team members. Organisations that develop the right mental health skills can make their teams more cohesive and resilient, which is much more likely to offer a competitive advantage.

The upward potential of investing in a wellbeing-intelligent workplace is also obvious. Work can boost wellbeing, and investing in workplace care is a vital asset. Studies show that individuals who are satisfied in their jobs are less likely to be absent from work and more likely to improve their work performance. And in some instances, high job satisfaction can protect against burnout and lack of engagement. In addition, those who feel happy at work are not only more efficient and effective but are also more cooperative, so they can support others and build a resilient work community. A sense of satisfaction at work can facilitate learning and teamwork,

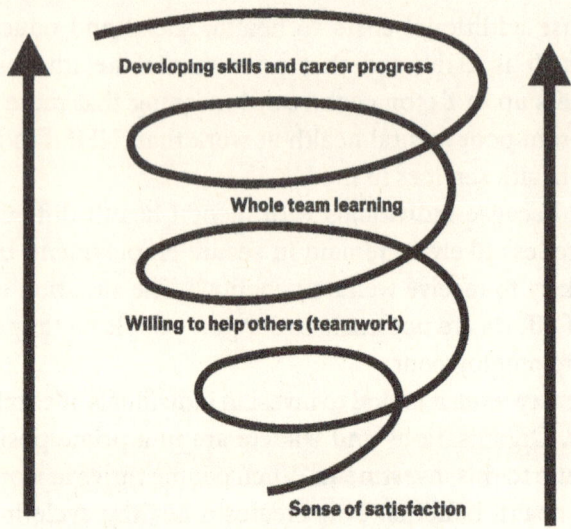

Figure 4: **The positive spiral of wellbeing benefits**

allowing individuals to develop and grow. This in turn causes a positive upward spiral, reinforcing our positive feelings at work. Figure 4 illustrates how wellbeing generates goodwill and feeds effort to support others, strengthening team learning and consequently individual and group development.

Positive work experiences also add value and meaning to people's lives. Engaging in work allows people to make use of their strengths and provides opportunities for challenge and growth. All these things create a healthy self-esteem, building resilience and support for times of distress. Good workplace wellbeing not only provides benefits in the present; it also supports the future.

American psychologist Abraham Maslow's theory of needs offers a visual approach to human motivation.[19] His hierarchy of needs is usually shown as a pyramid or ladder that individuals

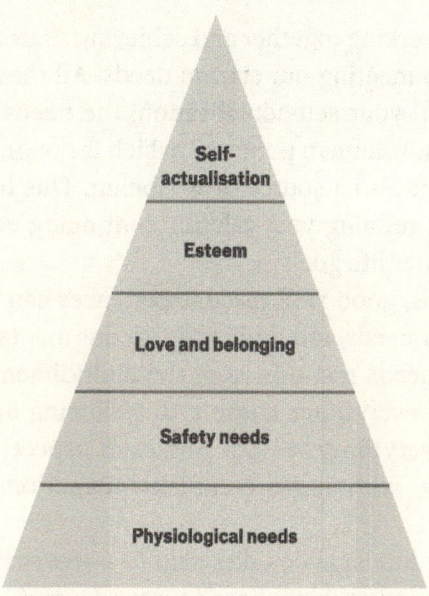

Figure 5: **Maslow's pyramid of motivational needs**

climb, and identifies the factors that they need to grow and thrive (see Figure 5). Positive wellbeing at work supports people's ability to make their way up Maslow's hierarchy; wellbeing intelligence is often about identifying what needs are not satisfied. Maslow's "ladder" helps organisations and individuals think about why they struggle to find the motivation to grow and experience positive self-esteem when more basic needs such as a sense of safety or love are not fulfilled.

At the base of the pyramid, being employed on a fair basis provides the resources to meet basic physiological needs: food and shelter, the most basic human survival needs we all require. As people move up the pyramid, work can help to accomplish our safety needs by providing financial security. It can also foster a sense of belonging, a feeling that you are part of a community, working together and achieving shared goals. Work is also vital in meeting our esteem needs. All these lead to the ability to fulfil your self-actualisation, the needs you meet to reach your whole human potential, which is not only a source of motivation but also a source of wellbeing. This includes skills development, refining your talents, continuing education and meeting broader life goals.

At all levels, good workplace experiences can be beneficial to our growth needs and, indirectly, to our mental health. The hierarchy of needs reminds us of the multidimensional nature of wellbeing: everything matters to wellbeing and wellbeing matters to everything we do. But each aspect matters in a different way, with more complex interactions than often assumed.

Wellbeing intelligence takes skill to uncover the sources of any wellbeing issues, how those sources depend on each other, and how to address them analytically. What follows will provide readers with the analytical tools to understand and address these issues practically at work.

2

Four mental health challenges at work

Remember Estephania, watching her team members disengage from their work? She feels they no longer have any enthusiasm or energy. And she is herself feeling deflated by the combination of work challenges and personal ones. She does not even know where to start. We would advise her to approach this as a clinician: the first step in addressing an issue is to recognise and understand what is happening. And that means understanding the core mental health challenges that she and her team members might be facing.

This first step is not easy because everyone's mental health and working life experience is unique. However, Estephania would probably feel much more confident about her ability to understand others' situations if she knew about the four most common wellbeing challenges in the lives of working-age adults: stress, burnout, anxiety and depression.

This chapter describes each of these challenges and their associated symptoms. The aim is not to provide a diagnosis but rather to aid awareness and recognition of when wellbeing is at risk. It is not uncommon for these symptoms to overlap and even feed each other. For example, stress can lead to anxiety, and vice versa; in most cases, it won't be easy to categorise the issues or to isolate them. The tables we provide below are a useful guide, but be aware that issues might be covered across many tables at the same time.

Stress

Stress is a very common experience. In fact, it's a normal and healthy response to everyday pressures or events that affects almost half of the workforce.[1] For example, you may feel stressed if you're due to give a presentation in a team meeting. Some of this stress may be useful; it may prompt you to prepare and be ready to answer any question. However, excessive stress may become unhelpful; if you are so stressed that you can't concentrate or remember what you're supposed to do or say in your presentation, that stress hinders performance. If the idea of presenting at the meeting becomes too much, to the point that you feel physically unwell or have the urge to run away, you're experiencing a very common and natural "fight or flight" response to what you perceive as a threat, even if that "threat" is a looming deadline or a presentation rather than anything that might endanger your physical wellbeing.

When this stress response is activated, your body will work hard to protect you by staying on high alert to deal with the danger. This happens in one of four ways.

1. Fight

If your body believes you can conquer the perceived threat, you will respond in fight mode. This means your body and mind prepare for the physical or verbal demands of combat. In the case above, you will go to this meeting with an "I can do it" spirit, but you'll stay on the defensive, ready to defend your ideas aggressively. In the workplace, the fight mode can be seen in the argumentative or hostile colleague who gets irritable when stressed.

2. Flight

If your body does not believe you can overcome the threat, you could respond by fleeing from the danger. Physiologically, in flight mode, people experience an increase in adrenaline, so that they can run for longer than usual, away from danger. Though you are less likely to literally run away from work, you may start to avoid or retreat from work stressors – think of the colleague who stops looking at or responding to emails in times of high demand. In the example of the stressful meeting, you might feel physically sick on the morning of the presentation.

3. Freeze

When your body doesn't believe you can fight or run away from the stress, you can freeze or feel stuck in the presence of a threat. The freeze response can be very common in workplaces. Often when you feel overwhelmed with multiple tasks and deadlines, you can't decide or prioritise which task to start first, and you end up not doing very much. When you freeze, it can be very difficult to make decisions and take action; unfortunately, this indecision leads to even greater stress. When you come to give your presentation at the dreaded meeting, you might struggle even to start.

4. Fawn

Fawning in the face of stress is an attempt to appease or minimise the danger of threat. Fawning typically presents itself in those who avoid conflict and are quick to ignore their own needs. At work, you may recognise a fawn response in those who people-please, say yes to every demand asked of them, and are quick to offer help even when not asked. On the surface, this colleague is a team player and a great asset to the organisation. However, in the long run, they are at high risk of burnout as they are unable to prioritise themselves or their needs. This situation could happen if the idea of having to present at the meeting lingers with you for days beforehand, preventing you from doing anything else.

The stress response has developed through years of evolution, and although you're more likely to be facing a difficult colleague than a sabre-toothed tiger, you still respond to any potential stressor in the same way. Your stress response is not fixed but may change depending on the perceived threat, the situation you're facing and the level of stress you're feeling at the time. For example, some people may find themselves fawning when their boss is making a demand, yet fight if a peer asks them to do something.

What does stress look like in the workplace?

Although people respond to and experience stress in different ways, there are several physical and tangible symptoms and experiences that are associated with stress that you can learn to recognise in yourself and others.

The most common physical manifestations of stress are headaches and increased tension, difficult digestion or stomach pains, feeling overwhelmed, and struggling to concentrate or to make decisions. In this sense, stress is *disabling*: it prevents you from expressing your full potential at work. Workplace stress is also likely to seep into your out-of-office life. Appetite, sleep, sexual life, your relationships with others (such as your degree of patience with partners or dependents) can all be affected by stress.

For many, stress will also lead to what psychologists call *coping behaviours*: excessive alcohol drinking or substance use, but also sometimes compulsive behaviours – for example, mindlessly scrolling through your favourite social media channel.

The worst part of stress is the snowball effect: stress accumulates, and some consequences of stress only reinforce it. Feeling overwhelmed, excessive worry, difficulties to disconnect and coping behaviours will make stress feel even more unbearable and disabling.

How to recognise stress in the workplace

Everyone has a personal understanding and experience of stress, so you might assume you can recognise it in other people reasonably easily. However, this is only sometimes the case, so you need to think carefully about likely symptoms. For example, you may recognise stress in the ways people communicate or relate to each other: your former easy-going colleague might start snapping at others or be described as having a "short fuse". They may also complain about being physically tired which can, in many cases, be a cry for help.

There are also behavioural signs to look out for. People under stress may snack more during the workday, take more smoking breaks or have an extra glass or two at after-work drinks. A stressed colleague may also struggle to complete or focus on their tasks. You may notice that they are working late or through their breaks just to catch up and finish their jobs. Or they may consistently arrive late to meetings because of forgetfulness or feeling overwhelmed.

Isaac, for example, is an electrician who has his own business. He visits his clients and helps them solve problems with their homes or businesses. He gets a lot of fulfilment and satisfaction from his job and loves the connections he makes

TABLE 1 **Common symptoms of stress**

Headaches and muscle tension in the body

Gastrointestinal problems
Including difficulty with digestion or stomach pains

Loss of sexual desire

Difficulty concentrating or indecision
Struggling to choose the next course of action, unable to focus

Feeling overwhelmed and struggling to take in information

Excessive worry, especially about worse-case scenarios

Forgetfulness
Struggling to focus and to remain attentive to tasks at hand

Irritability and quick to anger

Avoidance of others or specific places, especially those related to work

Changes in appetite
Eating more than usual, or skipping meals and having little or no appetite

Changes in sleep
Sleeping too much or too little, struggling to sleep or stay asleep

Overreliance on unhealthy coping mechanisms
Increased drinking, smoking, substance use etc., to switch off or unwind

with others. However, when one of his employees was on sick leave, his workload increased dramatically because he had to serve more of his clients himself. As a result, he was getting progressively more stressed. Isaac started to recognise that he was not as patient as usual; he also arrived late because of the extra appointments, and was feeling a bit overwhelmed. He had started smoking again as a form of stress relief and, when getting into bed at the end of the day, Isaac noted that his body was very tense as he lay awake worrying how he would get through the next day's work.

Isaac's experience is not unusual. But he was able to spot

the changes in his own behaviour and experience of work, and that awareness helped him to break the cycle. He decided that the next time one of his employees was unwell, he would try to re-schedule appointments or employ some temporary help so that he would not be caught in a vicious cycle of stress in the future.

Take a moment to think about your own stress response. Does your body feel tense at the end of a long day? Do you snap or get irritated by others quickly? Have you been obsessively engaging in a behaviour that takes your mind away from work, whether by alcohol or binge-watching television? It might well be the start of an addiction caused by your stress. Recognising why you engage in such behaviour is the first step to breaking the vicious cycle of stress. It will also help you to look out for signs of stress in others.

Burnout

Though not a traditionally defined mental disorder, burnout is a widespread and grim reality for many at work. It's often an inevitable result of rising work demands and a lack of resources and support. In stressful professions, such as nursing, burnout can affect more than a tenth of employees.[2] A global study of knowledge workers also found that 70% had experienced burnout.[3] But it's not all doom and gloom; burnout can often be the wake-up call that people need to assess their current situation and think about what exactly they need right now. Maybe your workload is unmanageable. Have you had a chance to have a break? Are you stretching yourself too thinly? Maybe you need more support in your life.

What does burnout look like?

Some of the warning signs and symptoms of burnout are the same as for stress: for example, the feeling of being physically, emotionally and mentally drained to the point of exhaustion. But, with burnout, the feeling of being overwhelmed and of loneliness becomes too much, often culminating in helplessness, feeling stuck and detached, and accompanied by a strong sense of self-doubt. Burnt-out individuals will also be left with a negative outlook. In this sense, burnout may present more like depression.

In contrast to stress, burnout is often a *threshold*. Beyond this threshold, it becomes impossible to focus and work, and a full reset is needed. Think about an overheated computer: beyond a certain point, it just shuts down.

How to recognise burnout in the workplace

Individuals experiencing burnout may begin to detach from the rest of the team as they lack the energy to engage with others. They may avoid attending meetings and any communal spaces. They may struggle to commit to doing their work as they procrastinate or put off certain tasks. Burnout may also present itself physically, with individuals looking physically exhausted or deflated; their posture and facial expressions might convey their exhaustion. Burnt-out people may struggle to take in new information and make decisions as they lack the mental capacity needed to process information. It might cause people to panic visibly as they get overwhelmed. Unsurprisingly, people suffering from burnout are incapable of functioning and tackling their usual daily tasks.

Even people who monitor their mental health and know all too well the symptoms of burnout might fall into the burnout trap. When people feel that their work is particularly meaningful,

TABLE 2 **Common symptoms of burnout**

Feeling tired and/or mentally, physically and emotionally drained
Feeling helpless, trapped or defeated Not knowing or believing there is a way out, feeling stuck and believing there is little chance for change
Feeling detached and alone in the world Not feeling able to reach out to others
A negative outlook about self, others and the future
Self-criticism and self-doubt, leading to feeling worthless or not good enough
Procrastinating and taking longer to get things done Putting off tasks, struggling to get started and not finishing tasks
Feeling overwhelmed

they can get so engrossed in it that they forget about their own needs.

Arnold, a newly qualified psychologist, was excited to start working for an eating disorder service. After an initial settling-in period, he was keen to take on further responsibilities and develop his clinical skills. As a result, he was appointed as a pathway lead responsible for assessing all under-25s who entered the service within two weeks of their referral. Arnold found this an exciting challenge at first; however, as referrals increased, it became more and more difficult to meet expected targets, and very quickly the deadlines became unmanageable and unrealistic. Many of Arnold's colleagues were also stretched and overworked. Because everyone's experience was the same, the service had developed a culture of "just get on with it and don't complain".

Over time, Arnold's stress and anxiety about his workload turned into feelings of mental and physical exhaustion. He began to feel resentful towards the service and started to avoid his colleagues, often turning off his camera in virtual team meetings and excluding himself from the group work chat. As a result of his experience, Arnold was left feeling hopeless about his work situation and fearful of taking on further responsibility in the future, despite how meaningful his work was for him. He had reached the threshold of burnout.

Anxiety

Anxiety disorders are among the most common mental health difficulties experienced by working-age adults. While some studies estimate that anxiety disorder might affect roughly 300 million people globally (4% of the global population),[4] work conducted during the 2020–22 pandemic found even higher levels. The level and frequency of fear and worry has also amplified in line with the rise in worldwide uncertainties, including climate change and geopolitical risks.

Many of the symptoms of anxiety are similar to those of stress: for example, fatigue, difficulty in concentrating, physical tension, irritability and sleeping and eating problems.

But anxiety affects people's working and personal life in a slightly different way to stress. Anxiety is fuelled by excessive, disproportionate worry that is difficult to control – the constant expectations that something bad will happen. Consequently, anxiety makes people feel restless, nervous and continually on edge. People who are anxious struggle to take time off and relax, which affects their ability to be productive and connect with others.

How to recognise anxiety in the workplace

People experiencing anxiety in the workplace may start to change their behaviours and interactions with others. You may notice they stop or are hesitant to contribute in team meetings and put forward new ideas. They may ruminate on specific tasks they have not previously had difficulty with. They may struggle to complete their workload in the same timeframe as usual, as they double-check or second-guess what they do.

Like stress and burnout, anxiety may also present physically. Someone may look visibly tired and distressed, and may also appear breathless and struggle to sit still, fidgeting during meetings. The pressure may also become apparent in their interpersonal relationships at work. They may be less likely to engage in topics that are not work-related, become easily irritated by other members of the team, and occasionally snap or respond angrily.

When someone feels anxious, they may start to seek reassurance and engage in safety behaviours (see Chapter 4). This could include asking others to review their work to make sure there are no mistakes, even after they have checked and rechecked themselves. Highly anxious people at work may also express a desire to have closer supervisory support than is necessary as they begin to doubt their capability. Alternatively, an overly anxious colleague may adamantly defend their right to do all their work themselves for fear of being judged, and spend lots of time outside work over-preparing.

Despite everyone's best intentions, anxiety at work can easily get out of control, especially in contexts that are particularly prone to it. Fiona, an experienced mental health nurse, works in a secondary care service. The service had recently received extra funding, and therefore a series of rapid transformations were taking place in what had been a steady workspace. As a result, her management failed to define the boundaries of her job clearly. However, as a mental health nurse, she was responsible for the most medically and psychiatrically risky patients. Because of the many changes, there was no clear support structure in place, and supervision was patchy at best. Supervision and line management were often cancelled at the last minute and unlikely to be rearranged. She could not get the guidance she needed.

Because of this, and despite all her experience, Fiona started facing work-related anxiety. She felt de-skilled and insecure about her ability to do her job. She began to seek reassurance by asking other colleagues to check over her work and would often copy senior staff into her emails just in case. She often over-prepared for meetings and worked after hours to finish her daily tasks to try to counter some of her anxiety. Overall, this left Fiona feeling exhausted and unhappy at work, which ultimately resulted in her changing jobs and the service missing out on her expertise.

TABLE 3 **Common symptoms of anxiety**

Excessive, disproportionate and difficult-to-control worry about events or activities Worrying about lots of different things. Struggling to stop or control the worry, or feeling as though something bad is going to happen
Feeling restlessness, nervous or on edge Struggling to relax and switch attention away from the worry or fear
Easily fatigued and often feeling tired
Difficulty concentrating and struggling to keep your attention on tasks (both work and leisure activities)
Irritability or getting annoyed and cross more often
Muscle tension – e.g. high shoulders, tense jaw, furrowed forehead
Sleep disturbances Difficulty falling or staying asleep; waking up in the night and worrying
The anxiety, worry and physical symptoms cause significant distress and/or impairment in social, occupational and other important areas of functioning Struggling to participate in usual activities, e.g. increased social isolation or missing work

Depression

According to the World Health Organisation, depression is the primary cause of disability worldwide, affecting approximately 5% of the adult population.[5] Unsurprisingly, it is very likely that depression or low mood will make its presence felt in the workplace.

Symptoms of depression are numerous and can differ from the symptoms of anxiety, stress and burnout. A useful reference point can be found in the UK's National Institute for Health and Care Excellence (NICE) guidance for identifying, treating and managing depression in adults, summarised in Table 4.[6] Some symptoms will be easy to spot in others, such as changes in weight and physical fatigue. However, some may be known only to the person concerned, such as low mood, diminished interest, disturbed sleep, feeling of worthlessness and poor self-esteem. In extreme cases, depression can lead to thoughts of suicide or self-harm which might be shared with others as a cry for help. Familiarising yourself with the common indicators of depression will help you to build your awareness and knowledge of mental health in the workplace.

How to recognise depression in the workplace

People with low mood or depression may show signs of distress in their interactions with their work and peers. They may limit their interactions with other team members as they begin to lose interest in the social aspects of the workplace.

They may become increasingly isolated and reserved at work and, like people with anxiety, they may stop contributing to team meetings or find ways to avoid them altogether. People with depression often struggle to keep up with their workload as they lack the energy to complete their usual tasks. Their feelings of worthlessness or not being good enough may mean they do not believe they can do their usual work and this can result in avoidance and an increase in employee absences. Significantly, this may also hinder their ability to ask for help.

It may also be possible to recognise depression from physical symptoms. You may notice individuals rapidly losing or gaining weight or complaining of being excessively tired. It is also possible that someone who is depressed may begin to talk about not wanting to be here, finding it hard to cope, or struggling to understand the point of work or life. In these instances, the individual is providing an insight into their current mental distress.

Causes of depression can come from outside the workplace, but they may be most visible at work because that's often where people interact with others the most. Harriet, a project manager, was struggling with a recent relationship breakdown. She hadn't shared this with any of her colleagues or friends at work and felt that she could forget her troubles by focusing on her job. However, although work was initially distracting and helped Harriet to cope, she found that this didn't last and she soon was ruminating about her relationship there too. She noticed her mood started to dip; as a result, she kept to herself and found that, even when she was with her colleagues, she didn't enjoy their company as usual. Even though Harriet was spending more time at her desk, she wasn't able to complete tasks and found herself procrastinating because she couldn't focus on what she was doing. Harriet felt that this meant she was bad at her job, which exacerbated her feelings of worthlessness.

TABLE 4 **Common symptoms of depression**

Low mood
Persistent feelings of sadness, anxiety or empty mood

Diminished interest or pleasure in activities
Finding it hard to engage in things that were previously enjoyable

Significant changes in weight or appetite

Significantly disrupted or excessive sleep
Struggling to get up in the morning or to wake up. Difficulty falling asleep, waking up in the night, and experiencing broken sleep

Agitation or slowing of thought and physical movement
Being fidgety or restless, struggling to sit still. Or feeling heavy in your body and moving more slowly than usual

Fatigue or reduced energy
Struggling to get things done because you don't have the mental or physical energy

Feelings of worthlessness or excessive or inappropriate guilt

Reduced ability to concentrate and sustain attention or marked indecisiveness
Struggling to make decisions, and procrastinating

Suicidal ideation, thoughts or acts
Thinking about death or dying or thoughts or acts of self-harm

From work pressure to anxiety and depression: connecting the dots

Feeling pressure at work is an everyday experience; everyone expects to feel a certain amount of pressure and it does not always translate into crippling stress. There are tasks to complete, bids to win, and clients to meet and work with. In some organisations, there is healthy competition between ambitious workers. However, when people experience intense pressure, typically because demands multiply with no break, they begin to feel stressed. Stress, in small quantities, is manageable, and in the short term can fuel ambition and make sure deadlines are

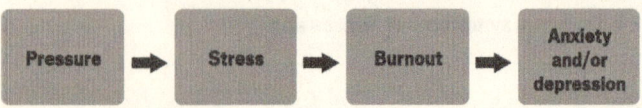

Figure 6: **The path to mental distress**

met on time. However, experiencing a chronic state of stress, with no respite or release, means that people cross the threshold into burnout. Therefore, prevention is the key to stopping the journey to poor wellbeing.

Figure 6 connects the different experiences of mental health discussed in this chapter: that pressure can lead to stress, that too much stress can lead to burnout, which can trigger crippling anxiety and depression.

Everyone has their own tolerance for pressure at work, so knowing when the pressure gets too much for oneself and others can be challenging. An early-career or entry-level employee, whatever their field, is likely to be more sensitive to pressure and more quickly overwhelmed than someone who has years of experiencing high-intensity pressure at work. It's the difference between a junior and a senior doctor or nurse, or between a junior analyst and a vice president at an investment bank.

Managers and leaders play a key role in building a culture where conversations about mental health are seen as acceptable and as the norm. Of course, no one is expected to understand and know everyone's pressure threshold at work. However, everybody would benefit from having the right conversations about capacity and mental strain. It's about creating a setting that allows people to reflect on their work environment and context. Managers and higher-level employees also need to lead by example. For example, if someone at the top is feeling overworked and under pressure yet continues to work regardless, they are communicating to the rest of the team that this is the way to work, this is how things are done and no matter how stressed or busy you are, you get your job done. Hardly inspiring. By reducing workload, taking breaks or sharing their challenges, more experienced and senior colleagues are communicating and validating that it's okay not to be okay, that "I am human and I am at capacity. This isn't a healthy way to work" and "My mental health is worth looking after – more than getting the job done."

Recognising your own stress threshold

How can you recognise when your own stress is building? The stress bucket analogy, created by psychologists Alison Brabban and Douglas Turkington in 2002, is a useful metaphor to understand and recognise our sources of stress, and to improve awareness of your individual stress tolerance (see Figure 7 on the next page).[7]

Imagine you're carrying a bucket around with you. Each time you encounter a stressor (be it a troubled relationship, financial problems, poor sleep or anxiety), your bucket starts to fill up.

As this continues, the bucket gets heavier and heavier. Some days, you may feel strong enough to carry the bucket and tolerate the stress, but other days it may be too much and you begin to feel the weight. One day you may find you get tired of holding all the stress; you've reached your limit, and the bucket overflows. You probably feel overwhelmed and mentally exhausted.

It's vital, therefore, to find ways to lighten the load. Imagine you're poking holes in your stress bucket to let the stress and tension leak out. These holes in the bucket can include taking breaks, meeting with friends to discuss things, or even getting a good night's sleep and meeting your basic needs. In this way, you can build resources to soak up the stress and avoid your bucket overfilling.

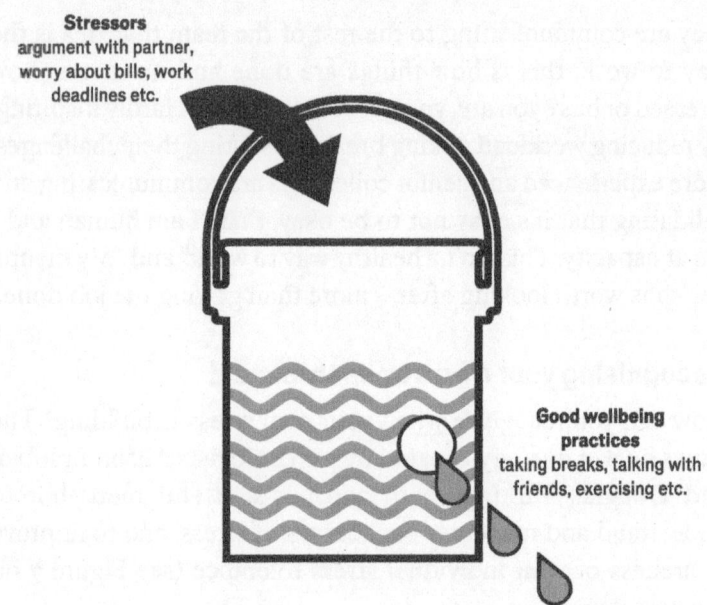

Stressors
argument with partner,
worry about bills, work
deadlines etc.

**Good wellbeing
practices**
taking breaks, talking with
friends, exercising etc.

Figure 7: **The stress bucket**

The mental health difficulties explored in this chapter do not provide an exhaustive list; problems of mental wellbeing are not limited to anxiety or depression, or indeed to any diagnosable mental disorder. Potential mental health challenges may not always feel like anxiety or depression; it may feel like loneliness following workplace bullying or insecurity stemming from imposter syndrome. Barriers to wellbeing may arise indirectly from poor team communication, lack of job security and workplace survivor's guilt. (We will cover these drivers, risk factors and mental health experiences in Chapter 6.)

However, it is useful to have a more precise understanding of stress, burnout, anxiety and depression, their prevalence in the workplace, and how they are all connected. Knowing the symptoms of those wellbeing challenges, how they overlap and interact, is the first step towards understanding when they affect us, and others. Take it as a compass to guide you through mental health matters. Recognition and the ability to spot mental health issues is a first foundational step to addressing them. They're the first step and the first skill of wellbeing intelligence.

3
Towards wellbeing intelligence

Gary has worked as the human resources director of a small family business for the last couple of years after a long career in human resources at a big corporate. During his annual review with his boss, Gary is being given the result of his 360-degree assessment. All his team members commend him for his capacity to listen, and two employees in particular have reported that Gary had been able to understand how their complex personal situations had affected their work. Gary had been able to help those employees with their mental health issues, and had supported their teams in a potentially difficult situation with minimal disruption.

Gary has always prided himself on being a good listener and tactful supporter of his employees. But it was the first time in his career that he felt recognised and appreciated for this. There was something he was doing right, and he wanted to be sure that he could understand it so that he could continue to support people and encourage others to develop these skills too.

It's no surprise that some crucial traits drive people's success at work. Gary, for example, was being recognised for his human and emotional skills in dealing with his colleagues. These days, it's accepted that there are many forms of intelligence in the workplace, including the numerical, reasoning and language intelligence (IQ) that are central aspects of problem-solving and communication. But, on their own, these cognitive skills are no longer considered enough. A core driver of performance resides in interpersonal skills, often encapsulated by the idea of emotional intelligence (EQ): the capacity to perceive your own emotions and the emotions of others and adapt your behaviours as a result. The concept is not new: it was forged by two psychologists in 1990[1] and popularised by writer and psychologist Daniel Goleman.[2]

While often labelled as an *interpersonal* skill, emotional intelligence is also an *intrapersonal* skill. It's as much about knowing your inner self and its working as understanding others. For Goleman, the first dimension of emotional intelligence is self-awareness: how you perceive, decipher and understand your own emotions and, importantly, what triggers them. This is about looking inwards and connecting emotions with their triggers, whether at work or beyond. On this basis, emotionally intelligent people can regulate their emotions. For example, if a manager exhibits a negative emotion, it can diffuse among colleagues and subordinates. But an emotionally intelligent manager will be aware of these negative emotions – and their effects on others – and look out for their triggers to help keep them in check.

Empathy for others often starts with self-awareness because emotional triggers and outcomes are likely to be roughly the same for people in the same work environment. In return, understanding what others are going through is a way to build your own self-awareness. In this sense, intra- and inter-personal skills are interconnected: they enable and reinforce each other. Gary, for example, has used his experience to understand what others might be going through. He has had multiple rough patches in his personal life and he remembers how it has affected his career and work.

Dealing with mental health (our own and others) in the workplace requires a good dose of emotional competence – both to detect and to address mental health issues with the necessary care. Gary could pick up on anger and frustration among team members when their colleagues were mentally unwell. And he could understand what those people were going through, which helped him to have the right discussions with them.

But although emotions and wellbeing are deeply interconnected, they have different scopes, definitions and implications at work. Emotions are less palpable and tangible: they are more diffuse, often hard to label (what is a positive or a negative emotion?), and their outcomes are not necessarily predetermined (will negative emotions always have negative implications?). Their effect on work is less direct than that of mental health, which affects both physical health and direct performance. We can experience a great range of emotions over a short period, with moods shifting depending on the context, people around us, or our thoughts. Wellbeing, however, is a longer-term state that influences behaviour and interactions in the workplace and beyond. Gary was not only great at picking up emotional cues, he was also willing to act on the underlying and lingering mental health challenges his employees were facing.

Emotional and wellbeing intelligence do have several crucial aspects in common. First, they are both about improving the work experience for oneself and others. Second, they are a skill that can be learnt and developed. Third, and most importantly, it's not only about connecting with others but also using our understanding of ourselves to connect with others.

Gary, quite clearly, has plenty of emotional intelligence. But he has also developed a good dose of wellbeing intelligence during his career. Although he can see the advantages of sharing those skills, he doesn't yet have the vocabulary to express what they are and how they might be used. He needs to have a better understanding of wellbeing intelligence.

Forging a new skill for the workplace: wellbeing intelligence

Wellbeing intelligence (WBQ) is a skillset and set of practical tools to help people understand and boost their own wellbeing and that of others. Since mental and physical health is becoming such a crucial driver of worker engagement and motivation, wellbeing intelligence, like emotional intelligence, has become a core competence at work. Detecting when others are struggling and knowing when and how to offer support is the crux of effective working relationships. And when everyone acknowledges the prevalence of mental health challenges, they can shift the organisational culture and raise awareness of this pressing concern. People at all levels can be depressed, anxious and stressed at work, but by recognising and addressing the root causes, they can demonstrate commitment to supporting the wellbeing of themselves and others.

Wellbeing intelligence, like emotional intelligence, starts with understanding and regulating yourself. By understanding yourself, you can then better understand and support others, whether they are colleagues, subordinates or peers.

Figure 8 on the next page summarises the essential skills that constitute WBQ. It's about identifying core mental health challenges such as stress and anxiety, acknowledging their root causes, and designing approaches to address them at individual, team and organisational levels.

The first step and first circle are focused on individuals: wellbeing intelligence starts with self-awareness. You need to cultivate your own wellbeing to help others. Self-awareness allows

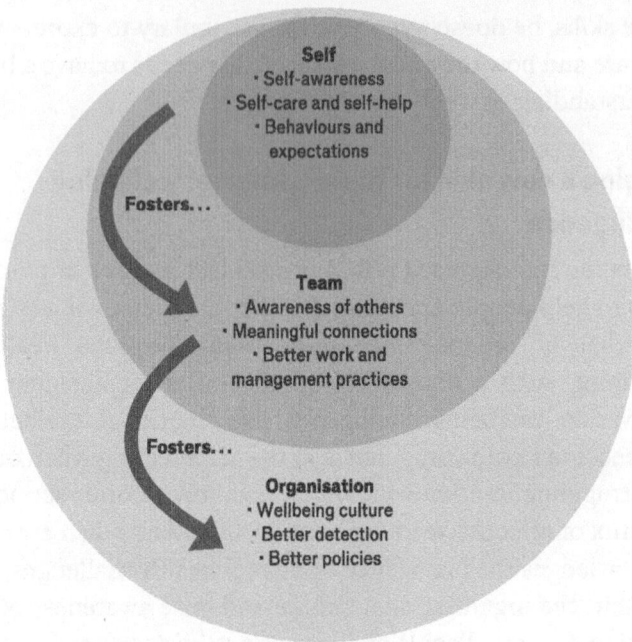

Figure 8: **The circles of wellbeing intelligence**

people to understand their thoughts, feelings and behaviours, and subsequently adjust individual work practices accordingly for self-care. It means reflecting on your experiences at work and identifying how they affect your wellbeing, positively or negatively. For example, you might reflect on what is driving a peak in anxiety and stress. Is it due to an experience at work, an interaction with specific colleagues, a tight deadline to be met?

Consider Gary's life story. He is no stranger to depression, which crippled him for a year in his early thirties after one of his siblings passed away. He disengaged from his job and quickly fell behind in his tasks. His awareness of others' wellbeing needs is rooted in this experience. He knows what it means to be struggling with work because of mental health and it makes him not just more vigilant, but also empathetic to struggling colleagues. When you experience a wellbeing-related struggle in the workplace, it is likely that others may face it too.

Self-awareness is like a sonar that can help you detect the wellbeing challenges experienced by others. And by acting on your own wellbeing challenges, you build a knowledge of what might work for others. Learning and addressing your own issues will also help you to develop a more systematic approach to disentangling wellbeing issues from their root causes. As you will see when we move to practical approaches to wellbeing, one of the core challenges of wellbeing intelligence is to understand what exactly causes the experience of stress or anxiety, which is a crucial starting point in addressing them.

Gary is also a reminder that wellbeing issues might not be attached to a specific experience at work but rather something outside the workplace. Differentiating those two types of experiences is a first step towards understanding what causes them and addressing the underlying issue. Wellbeing intelligence relies on continual self-reflection to make sure that you're meeting your own emotional and wellbeing needs before they grow too severe to ignore. Self-analysis enables you to make changes to work practices or structures that are causing problems.

Wellbeing-intelligent individuals are able to establish more meaningful connections with their colleagues, built on an understanding of how their wellbeing is affected by the work context. This approach also means that you can learn from experience, ultimately helping people to implement changes at the team level by focusing on better work and management practices. Gary has learned as much from the people he has helped as from the teams he has supported.

This team-level effort will broaden the support for wellbeing throughout the organisations by driving a shift in norms that might support a better detection system. It will also create momentum for new organisational practices and interventions. That's when change becomes systemic.

Developing wellbeing intelligence in practice: WBQ as a muscle

That may all seem pretty abstract. So how can we make WBQ a reality on the ground? Gary has a lot of tacit knowledge, and he wants to share it. He has derived know-how from his own experience, but he does not necessarily know why and how he was successful at dealing with those situations, and how he can continue to progress. This book offers a skillset and toolkit to apply WBQ in practice.

And you will need to practise. Wellbeing intelligence is not an innate skill. To become wellbeing intelligent, you need to learn a series of approaches to help you to understand mental health wellbeing and reflect on and refine your practices as you start to use them, and as organisation-level policies and practices (like regularly soliciting feedback about wellbeing from colleagues) develop too.

Wellbeing issues may take time to come to light and even more time to address. You will need an inquisitive and persistent mindset. But if problems persist, it's likely that the underlying root cause remains unresolved.

Another challenge for WBQ is the constant shift in work practices, structure and even in the design of jobs and collaboration. The shift to remote and hybrid working is an obvious example, but there are likely to be many more changes to come with the rise of new artificial intelligence tools and work technologies. The fact that most of us now interact with work colleagues – at least some of the time – over videoconferencing tools like Microsoft Teams or Zoom is just one example of how our working conditions are evolving. As a result, our approach to WBQ needs to evolve and adapt too.

Mapping wellbeing intelligence skills

Workplace intelligence goes beyond merely describing or diagnosing mental health issues at work. It's also about exploring what **people can concretely do about them.**

The WBQ skills we offer come from various models and techniques used by mental health practitioners that have empirically proved effective against distress.

The first circle of WBQ explores how individuals can build an understanding of their own wellbeing through a range of self-awareness tools, including tools focused on job design and work audits. It also looks at active approaches to self-care, such as mindfulness and grounding, and how to adapt behaviours and expectations to serve your own wellbeing better.

This understanding of one's own wellbeing can feed efforts to support team members and collaborators, in terms of both awareness and supportive practices. The second circle of WBQ is all about team building and check-in approaches to wellbeing, using relationship-building and nurturing methods anchored in cognitive behavioural therapy, which is one of the most effective approaches to mental health issues.

Wellbeing intelligence then informs organisational culture, policies and support practices. This third circle of WBQ looks at what makes a culture supportive of wellbeing intelligence, and the structures, strategies and interventions that organisations can put in place.

Table 5 on the next page summarises the wellbeing intelligence tools in this book and provides a map of the practical approaches you might take in different situations. Although this toolkit is not exhaustive, it should give you enough versatility to deal meaningfully with wellbeing challenges in the workplace.

TABLE 5 **Wellbeing intelligence tools**

Individuals	Relationships and teams	Organisations
Wellbeing self-awareness (Chapter 4) · Questionnaires · Hot cross bun diagram	Supporting awareness and connection (Chapter 6) · Team check-ins and check-outs · Non-work sharing · Wellbeing agendas · Risk assessment	Wellbeing culture (chapters 9 and 10) · Wellbeing leads and role models · Pulse surveys · Wellbeing culture audit
Wellbeing and work design assessment (Chapter 4) · Breaking maintenance cycles · Role analysis · Johari window · Work–life balance assessment	Tools to support the other (Chapter 7) · SMART goals · Wellbeing conversations · Behavioural activation across the working week	Policy (Chapter 10) · Regular job design assessment
Addressing personal wellbeing at work (Chapter 5) · Cognitive reframing and thinking styles · Behavioural activation · Worry time · Mindfulness · Grounding · Journalling · Further support checklist	Team dynamics and managing for wellbeing (Chapters 7 and 8) · Empathy maps · Motivation techniques · ARC model	Support (Chapter 10) · Integrating wellbeing in annual evaluations · Access to apps or online counselling · Hiring a mental health practitioner or outsourcing counselling support · Wellbeing training initiatives and workshops

The human, emotional and economic costs of poor mental health makes investing in wellbeing intelligence no longer optional. Because wellbeing is so closely connected to performance, reducing stress, anxiety and burnout might soon become a key performance indicator. Envisioning a future where people are routinely questioned about their mental health practices and the steps they have taken to enhance the wellbeing of their colleagues or team is not unrealistic. The competitive edge that Gary has built by developing his WBQ might soon be expected from most and become the norm.

In the following chapters, we offer key approaches used by mental health practitioners to assess and address wellbeing challenges and adapt them for the workplace. Gary might already be using many of these techniques, from reframing to cognitive behavioural therapy, but what follows will give him a deeper appreciation of why those approaches work, as well as giving him more strings to his bow. It shows you how to follow Gary's example and develop your own wellbeing intelligence.

PART 2

The first circle of wellbeing intelligence: self-care

"I'm just happy to be here." Tanya, a customer service representative for an insurance company, was discussing her experience of working during one of the waves of downsizing that her organisation experienced during a recession. Tanya worked three days a week from home at that time, but the guidelines on hybrid working were changing regularly.

For most of the week Tanya no longer worked in a shared office and therefore spent most of her workday alone, often on the phone hearing intimate details of people's tragedies when making insurance claims. Because of staff cuts, her workload had increased and she often had back-to-back calls throughout the day. Despite feeling increasingly low and overwhelmed with the volume of calls she was dealing with, Tanya felt she had no right to complain as she was one of the people who had kept their jobs.

Over time, Tanya began to dread going to work and often called in sick. When she was at work, she struggled to keep up with the pace of calls and this left her feeling worthless and unable to do her job. Tanya also noticed she began to overeat to help cope with her increasing stress, which ultimately led to feelings of shame and self-hatred, perpetuating her low mood.

Yet she could not put a label on what she was experiencing and, as a result, she and her colleagues felt unable to address it. Her experience, however, was shared by many others in that workplace and elsewhere. The problem had never been so prevalent, yet nobody had developed a clear understanding of what exactly wellbeing was, and what could help in times of distress, beyond slogans and umbrella terms.

To understand the wellbeing of others, the first step of

wellbeing intelligence is to distinguish and detect challenges in yourself, looking at what causes wellbeing challenges, and designing approaches to address those causes at a personal level. That means finding ways to assess your own wellbeing, and understanding and using the appropriate tools for self-care.

4

Assessing your own wellbeing

Understanding your own wellbeing and what drives it, is a fundamental element of wellbeing intelligence. But applying WBQ in practice requires a dedicated effort and a shift in mindset and habits: it means exercising self-care.

In practice, there are three core steps to enacting WBQ on a personal level.

The first step is *prioritising* individual wellbeing – an attitude that starts with looking inwards, and giving yourself permission to focus on your wellbeing. Prioritising means that you recognise mental health challenges at work and look to pinpoint their source. Without understanding what affects your own mental health, your potential to address other people's issues is limited. Striving to be an attentive, thoughtful, resilient and collaborative colleague means focusing on your own wellbeing.

In this first step, it's important to reflect on your experiences at work and identify how they affect your wellbeing, whether positively or negatively. For example, you might reflect on what is driving your current levels of stress. Is it related to specific interactions at work or specific periods, such as looming budget deadlines? Or is the experience one of a lingering sense of dread, typical of anxiety, when going to work? For Tanya, it would mean taking a moment to pause and reflect on why she is feeling the way she is, rather than forcing herself to perform when she's clearly not able to focus on her job.

The second step is about *building* self-awareness of your mental health through a more constant reflection. Wellbeing intelligence is not only for the challenging moments. It requires self-reflection to be a continuing process, rather than dismissing one's needs until they grow too severe to ignore. When Tanya is able to escape her vicious cycle of avoiding work and regain her ability to engage with and enjoy it, she will still have to keep an eye on her wellbeing. And if she can progressively build this self-awareness as a muscle, she will pay more attention to her state of mind and what might be influencing it, helping her to identify any future problems more quickly.

The third step is about *change*. Disengagement from work and vicious cycles of wellbeing generally have a clear cause, and mapping out causes and outcomes is a crucial first step towards making concrete changes. The self-analysis tools we provide in this chapter are about just that. In our own research into hybrid work, for example, we found that, when an abundance of meetings was causing increased stress levels, the wellbeing of senior executives benefited the most from a change that gave them permission to carve out time to focus and reflect on their own work.[1] By identifying and analysing the sources of their stress – in this case a lack of ability to carry out their own work because of overload elsewhere – they were able to come up with a clear solution. If Tanya can identify her sense of being overwhelmed and the absence of social support as the source of her struggle, she will be better placed to understand that the situation is not sustainable and to raise those issues with her manager. She will be empowered to make the changes and ask for support to do so.

In the rest of this chapter, we explore these three steps by sharing some core models and tools to help surface wellbeing issues, improve your wellbeing, and in particular break negative wellbeing cycles.

Prioritising your wellbeing

To prioritise wellbeing, you have to become aware of your inner world. This involves building your self-awareness and taking a conscious look at what you feel, what you do and how you think and relate to others. For example, reflect on how you feel when you have to go to work. Are there times at work when you feel happier? Or times where you feel uncomfortable? Thinking about your experience at the end of the working day can also be a useful barometer. Did you feel stressed, frustrated, underappreciated? Consider how you switch off or de-stress when the working day is done. By taking a deeper look at your experience with work you can start to understand yourself better.

Taking the time to reflect can make people feel vulnerable – so they tend to avoid it. But it can be all too easy to fall into bad habits or become ignorant of your wellbeing state. This is also common with physical health: you slip into periods of skipping the gym or sitting on the sofa all evening as soon as you come home from work. Or you might neglect nutritional needs and fall into a pattern of ordering an unhealthy takeout every night. The same can happen with mental health. People might feel low for so long that it starts to feel like normal. Work can be very busy so you expect to feel stressed and exhausted when you're there. There are also times when you don't realise you're under so much stress until your body tells you. For example, stress only becomes obvious when you can't sleep at night or you struggle with digestive issues.

Improving wellbeing therefore requires tools to develop self-awareness. Providing a moment to check in and reflect on your mood and how you're doing provides the opportunity to become more aware of your habits and the state of your wellbeing. When you become more aware of your inner world, you notice your thoughts and feeling, your moods and responses. You also gain more control over the possibility of changing or influencing the way you feel.

If you are new to thinking about your wellbeing, you may find it difficult or uncomfortable to pay attention to your thoughts or feelings. It might feel self-indulgent or even egocentric when so many people around you might also be suffering. You may have fallen into a comfortable pattern of avoidance, ignoring any difficult sensations or feelings that may arise. This is a very common experience; becoming aware of your inner world is a skill that needs to be honed.

Others may have been told (implicitly or explicitly) that they "should" or "should not" feel a certain way. Think of a young child having a temper tantrum: the busy parent is out grocery shopping for the family, the child sees a sweet or a toy they really want, and the parent tells them no. The child feels frustrated, and not having the vocabulary or capacity to verbalise this, goes into meltdown mode, screaming and shouting and not sure what to do with their anger. The parent tries to calm the child but they too are frustrated and respond in any way they can. Depending on how the parent responds, the child will learn about how their anger is received. If the parent shouts or punishes the child, the child may learn that it is wrong to feel angry. If the parent shuts down or goes silent, the child will learn "My anger is ignored, so to get attention (or love) I need to hide my anger." If, however, the parent accepts and understands the child's anger, the child will learn that "my anger is accepted; it's okay to be angry." In ways like this, you may have been "educated" to disregard your own feelings and emotions.

It may seem strange to place so much focus on early experiences when you're thinking about wellbeing in working adults, but much of your early experience can shape how you navigate and respond to emotions or difficult feelings. If you look even more closely, you'll find a whole range of examples of direct or indirect messaging related to feelings at work. For example, think of the female board member who feels she must take care in providing feedback or displaying valid anger for fear of being labelled as the "bossy" or "aggressive" woman. Or look at the young male black teenager who is careful not to raise his voice so as not be labelled "an angry black teen". Whatever your experience of growing up and living in society, you have been fed messages that can unintentionally shape your relationship with your emotions. You may deny your experience or invalidate certain feelings not because of ignorance, but lifelong habits.

When building awareness, you will naturally start to reflect on past experiences and relationships. You may begin to notice patterns in your behaviours, relationships and interactions with others. People pleasers, for example, are people who have a strong inclination to please others, even at their own expense. A people pleaser might have grown up in an environment where their emotional needs were unmet or ignored. They may have had parents who were busy with other siblings or had other commitments that took a lot of their time and headspace away. If their parents were very stressed, the child may have unconsciously tried to make their parents' lives easier by minimising their needs and focusing on being unproblematic or unburdensome as possible. Although this habit of minimising needs starts within the parent–child relationship, it begins to be repeated in other relationships. As the child grows up, they become the easy-going friend who is happy to go with the flow. They don't mind which restaurant they go to, or if their friends are half an hour late, and are always happy to be the designated driver. When they begin work, they'll be content to work late when asked, and overall be ready to serve their organisation. But this will all come at the expense of the people pleaser's own needs, wants and, ultimately, wellbeing.

By becoming more aware of your emotions and patterns of behaviour you gain not only control but also compassion for yourself. The more self-aware you can become, the more empowered you will feel to meet your goals, find fulfilling connections and live the life you want for yourself.

Building self-awareness

How can you begin to build and assess your level of self-awareness? At work, both formal or informal tools can help you to understand how well you're doing your job – for example, written or verbal feedback on performance, either based on a specific piece of work or as part of a more formal annual (or more regular) review. This all helps you to become aware of your capability: what you do well, areas of improvement, how you interact with other people, all of which will develop your ability to do your job. However, these tools are not designed to help you develop an understanding of yourself and your overall experience of wellbeing.

In the same way, while the assessment of job performance can rely on tangible indicators, such as sales made or customer satisfaction scores, wellbeing and mental health have their own metrics. Many of the assessments already used in a therapeutic setting can be adapted to help people reflect on their mental wellbeing at work.

One of those most recognised and empirically validated tool is the PHQ-9: the depression module of the patient health questionnaire. Behind this mysterious acronym lie nine questions that enable a well-rounded assessment of mental health, designed by Kroenke, Spitzer and Williams (see Checklist 1).[2] The questionnaire aims to screen and assess the severity of depressive symptoms and low mood. It is now one of the most widely used measures in clinical settings and it can be used to assess mental health difficulties – specifically low mood.

The PHQ-9 is highly adaptable to the workplace and can be used easily as an awareness tool for yourself and others. It contains a list of symptoms that people can experience when feeling low or depressed. Some questions focus on the behaviours you might see when you're depressed, such as sleep difficulties or appetite changes. Other questions focus on the thoughts you might have about yourself or others – for example, having self-critical thoughts when you make small mistakes.

CHECKLIST 1 **PHQ-9: the depression module of the patient health questionnaire**

Over the last two weeks, how often have you been bothered by any of the following problems?	Not at all	Several days	More than half the days	Nearly every day
1. Little interest or pleasure in doing things	0	1	2	3
2. Feeling down, depressed, or hopeless	0	1	2	3
3. Trouble falling or staying asleep, or sleeping too much	0	1	2	3
4. Feeling tired or having little energy	0	1	2	3
5. Poor appetite or overeating	0	1	2	3
6. Feeling bad about yourself – or that you are a failure or have let yourself or your family down	0	1	2	3
7. Trouble concentrating on things, such as reading the newspaper or watching television	0	1	2	3

8. Moving or speaking so slowly that other people could have noticed. Or the opposite – being so fidgety or restless that you have been moving around a lot more than usual	0	1	2	3
9. Thoughts that you would be better off dead or hurting yourself in some way	0	1	2	3

Scoring: Users score each item according to the frequency of symptoms, from "Not at all" (0 points) to "Nearly every day" (3 points). The total score gives an indication of the severity of depression: 0–4 no depression, 5–9 mild, 10–14 moderate, 15–19 moderately severe, 20–27 severe depression.

Give it a try. Take each question and score yourself honestly on each aspect. This will give you a sense of where you stand. It's also helpful to get a sense of how you are shifting from one part of the spectrum to the other. Context matters and you might score much higher after a difficult day at work than on a Sunday evening before returning to work. For Tanya, a weekly "self-check" using this questionnaire could help her awareness of how her situation might change and whether she is sliding down the path towards depression. Armed with this knowledge, she could then take steps to address her issues before they become too serious. High scores need the kinds of action we explore later in the book.

Whereas the PHQ-9 is focused on depression, the seven-question generalised anxiety disorder assessment (GAD-7) is used to detect the presence and severity of generalised anxiety as a specific mental health difficulty. GAD-7 is also used extensively across many clinical settings to assess wellbeing and can be helpful when trying to distinguish between typical levels of stress and excessive and problematic worry. Like the PHQ-9, the GAD-7 (see Checklist 2) asks people to rate specific behaviours (which are often much easier to self-assess than emotions or feelings, although the former are a direct consequence of the latter), such as difficulty relaxing or becoming irritable, as well as reflecting on thought processes, such as constant rumination.[3] The GAD-7 can be useful at work because it can help respondents to identify whether their worry is limited to specific work-based circumstances or if their worry is following them home.

CHECKLIST 2 **GAD-7: the generalised anxiety disorder assessment**

Over the last two weeks, how often have you been bothered by the following problems?	Not at all	Several days	More than half the days	Nearly every day
1. Feeling nervous, anxious or on edge	0	1	2	3
2. Not being able to stop or control worrying	0	1	2	3
3. Worrying too much about different things	0	1	2	3
4. Trouble relaxing	0	1	2	3
5. Being so restless that it is hard to sit still	0	1	2	3
6. Becoming easily annoyed or irritable	0	1	2	3
7. Feeling afraid as if something awful might happen	0	1	2	3

Scoring: Users score each item according to the frequency of symptoms from "Not at all" (0 points) to "Nearly every day" (3 points). The total score gives an indication of the severity of anxiety: 0–4 minimal anxiety, 5–9 mild, 10–14 moderate, 15–21 severe anxiety.

As with the PHQ-9, the GAD-7 helps people to assess their experience quantitatively and assess potential progress towards a more serious wellbeing challenge.

Both the PHQ-9 and GAD-7 can be used at work. We would

not expect or recommend that managers administer the scales, share anyone's individual scores or try to interpret them. But the scales can be made available for private and personal use as reflection and self-awareness tools. They build awareness of mood, provide a snapshot of immediate wellbeing and help people to focus attention on the here and now. Using the questionnaires regularly helps people to understand and recognise mood over time, progress and change, which, considering how subjective wellbeing can feel, can be difficult to measure. This can provide a valuable insight into how and when wellbeing is influenced by external sources (such as work deadlines or demanding customers). It can also prove useful when evaluating wellbeing interventions or resources in the workplace. For example, as we discuss in Chapter 10, companies can send out the questionnaires and request anonymous responses before and after workplace wellbeing initiatives to measure the effectiveness and impact of interventions on wellbeing, and refine them.

Using questionnaires such as the PHQ-9 or GAD-7 can be useful when you or a colleague are struggling to recognise how you or they are feeling. Many people, especially during a crisis or emotional turmoil, report feeling numb or removed from their feelings. This dissociation can be a coping mechanism, an attempt to protect themselves from the intense distress they may feel. Using a questionnaire can help direct attention back to their wellbeing and help them to focus and recognise hard-to-reach emotions of behaviours. Self-assessment is a step to bring themselves back to their experience and validate it.

Bringing change by breaking maintenance cycles

Wellbeing self-awareness is an engine for change, because it helps you to identify the source of wellbeing issues, and then target them to break a vicious cycle. An important tool to map out the causes and implications of wellbeing issues is the classic "hot cross bun model" or "four systems diagram" from cognitive behavioural therapy (CBT).[4] This model can be used to map out thoughts, feelings, behaviours and physical sensations. Figure 9 is an example of the hot cross bun model.

CBT uses the model to examine the interconnections between mood states (emotions and feelings), physical states (physical sensations in the body), cognitive states (thoughts and thinking processes), and behavioural states (actions and behaviours). The idea is that the different states can affect and influence each other. For example, when you feel stressed about an upcoming deadline, your worried thoughts and anxious

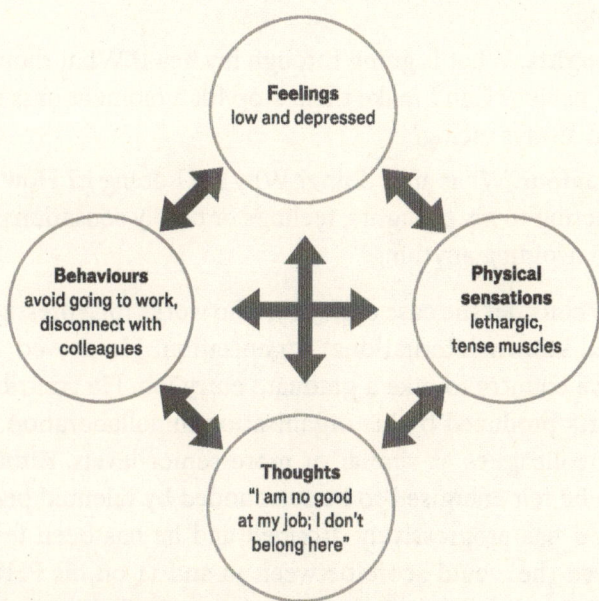

Figure 9: **The hot cross bun model: an example**

mind may prevent you from sleeping, and vice versa: when you struggle to sleep you are less likely to cope well with anxiety, causing a stress-filled feedback loop. The CBT hot cross bun model can help you identify the different areas of your wellbeing experience, and therefore increase awareness. The model can also encourage further reflection on areas that may previously have been ignored, such as behaviours or bodily sensations.

You can consider the connection between the states in any order.

- **Feelings**. What am I feeling right now? How would I describe my mood?
- **Physical sensations**. What's happening physiologically? Is my body tense (is my jaw clenched, are my shoulders high)? Am I breathing faster or harder than usual? Is my heart racing?
- **Thoughts**. What is going through my head? What thoughts am I having? Can I make them stop for a moment or is my mind always racing?
- **Behaviour.** What am I doing? Why am I doing it? How am I reacting to my thoughts, feelings or bodily sensations? Am I avoiding anything?

Let's consider the case of Bobby, who works for a prestigious and well-known international organisation. He moved from his home country to take a graduate entry job. He contributes to reports produced by his organisation in collaboration with various colleagues at similar or more senior levels. Although initially he felt energised to be surrounded by talented people, his mood has progressively dropped and he has been feeling depressed (he would score between 10 and 14 on his PHQ-9). While the feeling is obvious, Bobby has struggled to work out *why* he feels this way. Bobby can use the hot cross bun model to help him investigate his experience and pinpoint what causes it. In this case, by focusing on his thoughts, Bobby can see that he thinks his contributions are not as strong or useful as those made by his colleagues. They all have advanced degrees from prestigious universities and, in comparison, he doesn't feel good enough. Bobby can now understand that this feeling of inadequacy is what has demotivated him and made him reluctant to go to work or maintain meaningful connections with colleagues.

Hot cross bun maps can help to identify what psychologists call maintenance cycles. These are patterns of behaviour or thinking that fuel and maintain emotional distress. By identifying and discussing maintenance cycles, individuals can begin to recognise when they may be feeling stuck or repeating unhelpful patterns. In the workplace, typical maintenance cycles include avoidance, reduced activity and perfectionism.

Avoidance

This is common when experiencing anxiety. For example, many people worry about giving presentations, possibly because of how they will be perceived or a fear of public speaking. So they avoid giving them. In the short term, this alleviates their worry, but over the long term, it perpetuates their anxiety. The next time they have to give a presentation to a group, they will be just as anxious – and often the anxiety, fed by avoidance, is more intense. Bobby might well have experienced the same feelings, and his fear and anxiety mean that he will withdraw from those interactions that could reassure him about his contribution at work.

Reduction of activity

This is typical when experiencing depression and low mood. A manager may notice that an employee is not attending team meetings – or even struggling to come to work – and is disengaging socially. The maintenance cycle looks like this. An employee feels unappreciated or unfairly treated. The person decides to do less, which reinforces feelings of lethargy and disconnection. Bobby is indeed stuck in a cycle of doing less, which will make him feel less recognised and even more of an imposter.

Perfectionism

The need to perform at the highest level is often associated with low self-esteem or anxiety. When you believe that a task must be done perfectly, you might abandon tasks that you fear you cannot finish to that standard. Or you avoid even starting a task for fear of doing a subpar job. You feel paralysed and become even more concerned that only perfection is acceptable. Bobby might also have been experiencing similar feelings as he worries that he is not good enough.

When people find themselves stuck in maintenance cycles, they often engage with safety behaviours. Safety behaviours are actions which reinforce the maintenance cycle. They make you feel safer in the short term but prevent you from overcoming the source of distress, anxiety or stress in the long term. Disengagement from work, in the cases of both Tanya and Bobby, are typical safety behaviours, reinforcing their source of worry and ultimately getting them into a vicious cycle.

A typical example is people suffering from social anxiety at work. If they struggle to interact with colleagues, they decide not to see anybody and avoid others. They may begin to skip the work drinks or eat lunch on their own. While this will provide short-term relief, it will only aggravate the issue in the longer term. There is also the unintended consequence that people might stop trying to include their socially anxious colleague due to their avoidance, thus creating a self-fulfilling prophesy. In this case, deciding not to interact with colleagues is a safety behaviour that will often reinforce the maintenance cycle. Only by identifying the safety behaviours and breaking those cycles can individuals begin to reclaim their wellbeing.

It can be very easy to slip into a maintenance cycle, and, without awareness, you might find yourself stuck for a long while, as you can see in the example of Bernd. Bernd has been working as a developer at tech firm ZX for just a few months. A couple of weeks ago, he sent an email to his boss to ask for clarification on a project he was working on. The tone of the reply was cold and Bernd assumed that his email had reflected poorly on him: he assumed his boss now thought he lacked autonomy and could not manage a project on his own. Since then, he has been worrying excessively about asking his boss anything. He is overthinking and second-guessing his work. He regularly goes to his colleagues to ask them for their advice (a safety behaviour), even when they are unlikely to be able to help. But this reassurance behaviour does not help him face this issue and he becomes anxious about his electronic and face-to-face interactions with his boss. He progressively disengages from work, so now his boss becomes really concerned about Bernd's performance.

A simple discussion with his boss would have helped Bernd realise that he had read far too much into the initial email. However, because Bernd was engrossed in his safety behaviours, he struggled to find the space to reflect and fully understand the situation. Mapping out possible safety behaviours and why they emerge could help him see where and how to break this vicious cycle, as shown in Figure 10 on the next page.

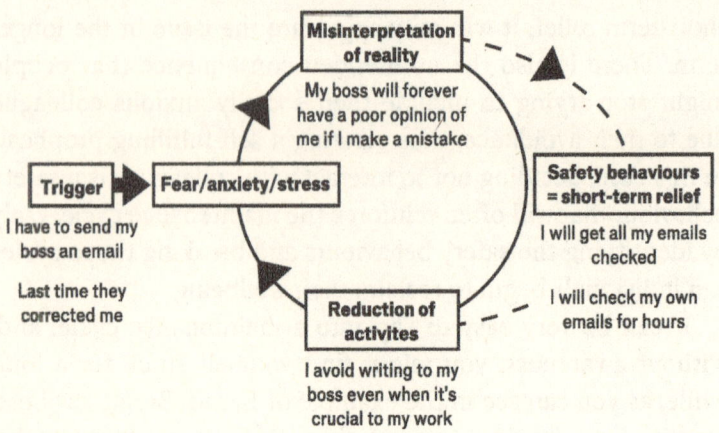

Figure 10: **A maintenance cycle example**

Redesigning work for wellbeing, together

Earlier, we described self-care and self-awareness as central pillars of wellbeing intelligence. On an individual basis, developing self-awareness leads to empowerment; those who are self-aware are better able to begin to take charge and responsibility for their wellbeing and mental state. And by encouraging self-awareness, managers can adapt their workplaces to create environments that support wellbeing and good mental health. Increased self-awareness can be used proactively within teams and organisations with the understanding that, ultimately, workplaces with better wellbeing intelligence will benefit not only individuals but also the whole organisation.

Another essential self-assessment tool is the Johari window. Developed by psychologists Joseph Luft and Harry Ingham (hence the name, Jo-Hari), the Johari window is a tool to improve understanding of the relationships you have with yourself and others.[5] It's where wellbeing intelligence meets work relationships: it turns the analysis towards the connections you build with others at work. In particular, it shows how others perceive you, giving you a more rounded understanding of your strengths and weaknesses.

It works by asking you and other people to provide reflections and feedback on your strengths, weaknesses and personal qualities. Typically, these attributes are taken from a list of adjectives and selected qualities that are then used to populate the four different sections of the Johari window (see Figure 11 on the next page).

The window comprises four quadrants of qualities and characteristics that an individual may possess from four perspectives.

1. **Open**. These are characteristics, behaviours or information that are known to you and to others. This information is usually freely shared and known – for example, your job title, role and qualifications.
2. **Blind.** These are qualities or traits that are known to others but not to you. For example, others may perceive you as being punctual or as a good team player but you may not see yourself this way.
3. **Hidden.** These refer to the knowledge or features that are known to you, but not shared with others. This may include your private history or personal thoughts and feelings.
4. **Unknown.** These are the traits, characteristics or information that are unknown to both you and others. These could include skills that have yet to be discovered or relationship qualities that have yet to be developed.

The Johari window capitalises on the knowledge and feedback from yourself and others to know yourself better: you can use the "collective mind" of your colleagues for your

1. Open Known to self Known to others	2. Blind Not known to self Known to others
3. Hidden Known to self Not known to others	4. Unknown Not known to self Not known to others

Figure 11: **The four quadrants of the Johari window**

self-assessment. It can be used within teams and workplaces as an exercise to build shared awareness. Team members can complete the window individually and then ask for and provide feedback to aid discovery and build trust with one another.

For example, college administrator Naomi was keen to move up the career ladder and develop her promotion prospects. To help understand herself and her approach to work she enlisted the help of her colleagues and completed a Johari window.

1. First Naomi populated the hidden quadrant of the window, writing down her personal qualities, strengths and weaknesses (e.g. ambitious, shy, scatty, generous, helpful, realistic).

2. Next Naomi asked for feedback from others, asking them how they found working with her, and what her strengths and weaknesses might be. Naomi reviewed this feedback and was surprised by some of the qualities mentioned. Naomi wrote down any new feedback from others in the blind quadrant (e.g. dependable, headstrong, accepting, responsible).

3. The characteristics that both Naomi and others mentioned were added to the open quadrant (helpful and realistic).

4. Naomi thought about the qualities or skills that had not been mentioned. She wrote these in the unknown quadrant (e.g. creative, authoritative, curious).

5. Finally, Naomi reflected on each of the quadrants separately and the window as a whole, reflecting on the traits that she didn't expect from the blind quadrant. Naomi also thought about how she could develop skills from the unknown quadrant that she hadn't yet explored, and if she would be willing to share with others any qualities from the hidden quadrant to understand herself better and develop her career.

By using the Johari window, self-awareness can become a team experience, a collective endeavour. Tools like these can also create a culture of feedback that builds trust and openness. The Johari window helps people to understand their hidden capabilities, and see themselves in a better light. Bobby would be well advised to engage in this exercise and he might well realise that many of his teammates experience the same imposter syndrome. By collecting feedback from his peers, he might realise that he has skills and expertise that are unique and useful to the collective, and that he deserves his seat at the table and his job in the organisation.

Role analysis

With better self-awareness, people may begin to notice their mood changes before or after certain work situations or events. For example, you may notice increased anxiety when working with particular individuals or getting closer to a deadline or performing certain tasks. Therefore, we also recommend using self-awareness to consider job roles in detail and to engage in *role analysis*. This is about reflecting on and potentially revising the scope and tasks included in a work role or job. It can also support wellbeing, as well as being a tool to assess work–life balance.

You can do this by reviewing your job description. Consider each task listed and how you would rate the tasks on their enjoyability and achievability. Ponder over the tasks and responsibilities listed: is the list accurate? There might be many things that are not listed in the job description and yet are central to your work. Where do you feel fulfilled or challenged? You can identify areas for which you struggle to complete tasks. Do certain tasks leave you feeling more exhausted than others? Or cause stress?

By reflecting in detail on your job description, you can consider all aspects of your role and the potential of these tasks to influence your mood positively or negatively. You can then use this to discuss your job with colleagues and your manager. It's also a technique that managers can use with their team members. For example, if someone really enjoys collaborating with others, a manager might suggest they take the lead on a team project or participate in a cross-functional team to promote a positive work experience.

Work–life balance

When thinking about the impact of your work on your wellbeing, it can be useful to reflect on how work corresponds and balances with the rest of your life.

We have created a *work–life balance assessment* to assess the impact of work on your wellbeing more generally. You can use this checklist formally or as a prompt for discussion or reflection on your relationship between wellbeing and work.

CHECKLIST 3 **A work–life balance assessment**

Ask yourself the following questions.

· How much time do you spend at work?

· How much work do you do outside your contracted hours?

· Do you take lunch breaks?

· Are you offered overtime?

· Is overtime paid or unpaid? (Formalised or ad-hoc)

· Do you take all your annual leave?

· Do you think about work at home? How often? What feelings come up?

· Are you contactable outside working hours?

· Are you expected to be available outside working hours?

· Is flexible or agile working available (and used)?

· Do you get enough sleep?

· Do you have to commute to work? How long does this take?

· How do other commitments fit around work?

· Do you engage in any networking for career purposes?

· How much time a day do you have to relax? Or to yourself?

· What other commitments do you have? And how do these fit with work?

When answering the questions, think about whether you would want to answer differently. Consider aspects covered by the questions that you have more control over and what more you could do to preserve your work–life balance.

When reflecting on your role, we're not simply suggesting that everyone stops working at 5pm on the dot. Or leaves the working world completely. We're encouraging you to consider how your work may help or hinder your wellbeing, the boundaries you have between work and life, and whether these need to change. Reflecting on your job is about making your career work for you and your lifestyle.

For some people, getting into the office at 7am works for them because it means they finish in the afternoon and can deal with childcare. For others, working from home one day a week means they don't feel distracted or sucked into meetings that feel unnecessary. Everyone will have a different approach to work and how it melds with their outside life. A young professional working in a hedge fund may appreciate out-of-hours contact because it provides a chance to network with industry professionals and connect with people in the field. Such extracurricular activities will not only build the young professional's connection with colleagues but also progress their career as they connect with mentors. In the same way, trainee employees may spend their evenings revising for professional exams hoping to develop their skills and promotion prospects or enable them to move into a field that gives them more meaning and satisfaction. In contrast, the experienced professional who has worked their way to secure a stable role will appreciate having built a working life that now supports their lifestyle.

This chapter has focused on the importance of self-awareness for self-care and offered some concrete tools to help you to know yourself better. The questionnaire and exercises can help you map out the *why* of any wellbeing issues, and *how* and *where* to start addressing them. Diagnosing maintenance cycles is often enough for people to start tackling the issues. But the boundaries of work and job tasks also need to be examined as they can be the source of severe imbalance and difficult relationships with colleagues and work. Tanya, Bobby and Bernd could all have used these tools to understand the reasons why they disconnected from work and from colleagues. Instead of feeling worse and worse, identifying what caused their wellbeing issues, and how they maintained and encouraged their negative feelings, could have helped them to build the self-awareness needed to take action to break out of those vicious cycles.

5

Tools for self-care

Asma owns a luxury real estate agency in the south of France. During her working day, she goes from one appointment to another, works for demanding clients and manages a five-person team, all while managing care for her older parents. Many people in this situation would feel consumed by their work, constantly overwhelmed or even burnt out. Asma's professional success and dedication to her parents could have derailed her. Yet they haven't.

The reason why Asma can juggle all of this is because she has set up her own routine of self-care. She sets clear boundaries between her work and personal life. She balances taking care of her parents and a full-on job with activities just for herself, like a run on the beach every day, seeing her friends every Saturday night and reading a book for an hour every night. This is about not only listening to herself, but also keeping some time to focus on herself; she is proactively exercising self-care.

Self-care is personal for everyone and can take many forms. For some, like Asma, self-care will mean waking up early at the weekend to go for a run. For others, it will mean having a lie-in to catch up on rest. Self-care can mean lots of different things and there is no right or wrong way to practise it. It will vary from person to person and will change over time.

Ultimately, engaging in self-care is an investment in the self. This is something many people may feel unfamiliar with or uncomfortable doing. They may feel that they don't have the time: other people are relying on them just to keep going. What they often don't consider is what happens if they become incapacitated because they have forgotten themselves for too long. Growing up you may have heard people who took time for themselves labelled as *selfish* or *lazy*. Or you may have chastised yourself for taking a break or holiday. You may have heard the classic "What have you got to be stressed about?" response from others. There is also a trend to wear exhaustion and burnout as a badge of honour: the "Look at me. I'm so busy and stressed" or "How do they do it all?" The reality is that these people don't do it all and they certainly can't sustain such high levels of stress and busyness without consequences. Something has to give, and it's usually wellbeing.

Many organisations and workplaces don't typically reward self-care. Goals and targets are based on achievement, and the purpose is to work, not rest. It can feel counter-intuitive to consider self-care in the workplace at all and even more so to recognise and incentivise it. However, encouraging self-care in the workplace benefits the organisation at all levels: individual, team, and the company as a whole. Self-care builds resilience and strengthens people's ability to cope in times of high stress. It can act as a protective measure to ensure that, when stress arrives, people are ready and can handle what comes next. As individuals, people can use self-care in times of distress as a way of managing difficult emotions and returning to a calmer state.

The first step to any self-care practice is to give yourself permission: permission to take time for yourself, to step away from work, caring responsibilities, family, children, parents – just for a moment. The next step is to let go of the myth that being extremely stressed is an achievement, because it's not: extreme stress is hard and damaging to your wellbeing and peace of mind. Remember the stress bucket mentioned in Chapter 2: everyone in life faces stressors, commitments, work to be done, and all the while that bucket is getting heavier and heavier as stress builds. Think of self-care practices as the holes you poke through the bucket to lighten your load. The following tools and self-care practices are based on methods used by psychologists and therapeutic practitioners to help you find ways to poke holes in your super-busy life and regain breathing space. We recommend you approach these tools with an open mind and remember that self-care practices require time and patience.

In this chapter, we start with the crucial shift from negative thinking, offering tips on how to challenge negative thoughts proactively. We'll then look at the behaviours and practices that enable wellbeing. By working on both your thinking and on your behaviours, you'll be able to build your capacity for self-care.

Self-care thinking

Nick is a secondary school teacher. He is always negative and pessimistic: he thinks the students don't like him, the parents don't like him, that he is terrible at his job, and that the government will make his life harder and harder. His is a typical case of negative thinking, and he has built quite the reputation at work, being known as "Negative Nick". But Nick can challenge those thoughts and reassess his conclusions with a healthy dose of objectivity. After reading this section, Nick will know how to consciously challenge himself when those negative thinking patterns emerge. And with a bit of luck, his colleagues will stop calling him "Negative Nick."

Everyone has different *thinking styles*. For example, some people may be more prone to optimism, believing that things will work out all right in the end. Others may have a pessimistic perspective and think of the worst-case scenarios. These different mindsets will have an impact on how people interpret the world around them, and subsequently how they feel about it. For example, imagine you are heading into the town centre on Saturday morning and looking for a parking space. If you are optimistic in your thinking, you will expect to find a parking space and feel relaxed. However, if you are pessimistic in your thinking, you will expect not to find a parking space and you'll most likely feel stressed about it even before you reach the car park. Though a very simple example, this demonstrates the ways in which someone's perspective or thinking can affect their wellbeing.

Reflecting further on thinking can lead you to discover your thinking styles and possible *cognitive distortions*. Cognitive distortions are negative thinking patterns that can cause or perpetuate mental distress or poor wellbeing. They are like "reality" distortion because they are fed by your fears and worries, presenting you with a misleading version of reality that only encourages negative thinking patterns.

In this section, we look at three key components for tackling negative patterns of thinking:

- how to identify those negative patterns
- understanding how they manifest in practice
- how to challenge them through what psychologists call "cognitive restructuring".

Identifying your cognitive distortions

What follows is a summary of 11 types of cognitive distortion that people commonly experience, together with alternative ways of thinking that might help you to challenge each one. Read through the list and consider which ones you might recognise. People can be subjected to multiple forms of cognitive distortion at the same time and on the same issue. For example, someone who is afraid of giving presentations in public or speaking up in a meeting might be experiencing an all-or-nothing distortion ("I always bomb it when I speak up"), overgeneralisation ("Each time I speak with my colleagues I feel so nervous") or should and must ("I should only speak up when I have a ground-breaking contribution to make"). This tends to exacerbate the negative feelings because their belief is confirmed repeatedly. If you recognise any of these distortions in yourself, write down the remedial approach and use it as an aide-mémoire.

All-or-nothing

All-or-nothing distortion is thinking in terms of absolutes – for example, using "never", "always", "everyone" or "all the time".

- I'm always stuck with the boring tasks.
- Everyone always ignores my input.
- I never get good feedback.

Alternative. Find the middle ground. Think of times that counter the absolute.

- I found contributing to the last report really interesting.
- They tend to ask for my point of view more often than not.
- I get a mix of positive and critical feedback.

Overgeneralisation

Overgeneralisation involves making broad assumptions and interpretations based on a single event, or on few events or little information. For example:

- I felt nervous speaking in that meeting

generalises to:

- I'm always so nervous.

Alternative. Be specific about the events you are talking about and look for situations that contradict the overgeneralisation.

- I was nervous speaking in that meeting, but I feel comfortable one-to-one.

Mental filter

This is focusing on the negative aspects while filtering out and ignoring any positives. For example, after a successful presentation, thinking:

- I couldn't answer all the questions asked of me after I presented my work.

Alternative. Consider the whole picture. Take time to consider both negative and positive aspects of events to provide a more realistic and balanced view.

- I couldn't answer all the questions, but those I did answer, I addressed very well.

Jumping to conclusions (also referred to as mind-reading)

This is over-interpreting the meaning of an event using minimal or no information.

- My boss didn't give me any feedback. He must think I'm not performing well.

Alternative. Slow down, don't make quick assumptions. Consider many alternatives to the first assumption you make.

- My boss didn't give me any feedback. Maybe he is busy, or maybe there's not much to work on (or not much feedback to give).

Disqualifying the positives

This is dismissing positive events as the result of good luck or chance rather than merit.

- I handled the client complaint well because the client was so easy going, friendly and nice.

Alternative. Acknowledge the positives. Reflect on the positive results and your contributions to them.

- I handled the client complaint well because I was calm and listened. I am really good at this!

Magnification and minimisation

This involves exaggerating or reducing the importance of events.

- Getting a pay rise isn't a big achievement.

Alternative. Do a reality check. Using evidence, try to formulate a realistic view of the event.

- I worked hard and managed to negotiate a pay rise. I did a good job.

Emotional reasoning

Emotional reasoning is assuming that because you feel something, it must make it true.

- I feel anxious about my presentation. I must be worried I will mess it up and look ridiculous.

Alternative. Feelings are not facts. Remember, feelings are valid but not always true.

· I feel anxious about my presentation, but I am safe. I know what I am talking about and this worry will pass.

Should and must

"Should and must" means thinking and believing that things should be done in a certain way (often resulting in overly critical and pressuring language).

· I should be able to finish all my work by lunch and will do whatever I can to make it happen.

Alternative. Flexibility. Take a self-compassionate approach and be open to other ways of doing things.

· It is unrealistic to expect my full day of work to be finished by lunchtime. I will do as much as I can.

Personalisation

Personalisation is the belief that you are always responsible for external events.

· My boss is always upset. She would be more relaxed if I was better at my job.

Alternative. Find the cause. Reflect on why you may feel personally responsible. Remind yourself that some things are out of your control.

· My boss might be upset because she's missing a family event for work.

Labelling

This involves assigning a label to one characteristic and using it to describe a whole person or yourself by it.

- I can't even get this one task right. I'm such a failure!

Alternative. Limit your judgement to the situation only; avoid generalising.

- I can't get this one task right, but I can do other tasks well.

Catastrophising

This is the tendency to blow things out of proportion and see only the worst possible solution.

- The customer left me a bad review. I'm going to get fired. My career is over!

Alternative. Put things in perspective. Try to introduce a realistic perspective to the situation.

- The customer left me a bad review. I might have to discuss this with management and make some changes.

Thought records: challenging negative thinking

People often fall into patterns of thinking without realising it, and without reflection, these ways of thinking become habits. Using *thought records* will help you to discover your cognitive distortions and thinking styles. A thought record is a simple three-step process to identify thoughts and feelings about a situation you might be facing. It connects the situation, the emotions you are experiencing, and your direct thoughts. These direct thoughts can then be re-evaluated to see how they might fit with a common cognitive distortion.

For example:

- The situation. My boss asked me (and no one else) to work late today.
- The emotions. Frustration. Anger. Worry.
- The thought. I'm not working fast enough. I can't get my work done in time. Maybe I'm just not good enough or I'm just lazy.
- The cognitive distortion. Jumping to conclusions and labelling.

Reflecting on what is felt and the content of the thoughts at work can uncover unhelpful thinking styles that are often automatic and unconscious (also referred to as *negative automatic thoughts* by psychologists).[1] Without reflection, we are prone to repeating and reinforcing them.

Once you have identified the cognitive distortions, it is possible to challenge and change your thinking (and improve your wellbeing) by using *cognitive restructuring* or *thought challenging*. The aim of thought challenging is to reflect on the interpretation of events to formulate an alternative and realistic perspective. Often, distortions are not grounded in reality but are a reflection of your distress and anxieties which then tend to fuel your distress and anxieties even more. Therefore, if you can uncover an alternative perspective that reflects the situation more accurately, you can increase your chance of thinking more positively.

In the following example you can see Ahmed moving through the steps of thought challenging to result in a shift in mood.

Step 1. Identify the unhelpful thought(s) and label the cognitive distortion

Ahmed is feeling stressed and exhausted as he juggles work with caring for his mother. He realises that he is feeling worried about how time off will affect workflow. He needs to zoom in on the negative thinking pattern causing this fear: "If I go on leave, no work will get done and I'll have so much to do when I return." Ahmed is also engaging in the *personalisation* type of cognitive distortion – taking responsibility for external events.

Step 2. Evaluate the thought

List the evidence that supports the unhelpful thought and the evidence that challenges it. Evidence can be objective or based on previous experience.

Ahmed can now scrutinise the negative thought for evidence that either corroborates or challenges it. This keeps him from uncritically accepting the thought and being drawn into a cycle of negative worry. He may consider evidence that he feels supports his concerns about work getting done. He may have received no offers of assistance, colleagues may not meet his work standards, and other team members may be on leave. But he can also try refuting the negative thoughts: No one is indispensable; the company's success does not hinge solely on his constant presence; colleagues have demonstrated the ability to produce quality work, and he has gone on leave before without any dent in his overall performance or interruption to his projects. Reflecting on the evidence for and against the unhelpful thought also enables Ahmed to find the cause of the personalisation cognitive distortion. He can reflect on the extent of his responsibility in running the organisation and consider if this is realistic or not.

Step 3. Form an alternative and more realistic perspective

Informed by this evidence, Ahmed can begin to frame his situation in a different light. "There may be a lot of work to do when I return, but I need and deserve a break and others are available to support me if I need them to." Holding on to unhelpful thoughts maintains the worry and triggers a maintenance cycle. However, by using cognitive reframing, Ahmed can develop an alternative perspective that is grounded in reality and enables a shift in his mood. Ahmed may now feel more confident and comfortable about taking a break, minimising the stress he feels he will have to carry.

Self-care behaviours

Just as thinking can have an impact on your wellbeing, behaviours and actions can influence your mood. And at some point, it is crucial to move from self-analysis to action. Wellbeing self-care is not just a matter of how you react to specific situations. You can improve your wellbeing on a daily basis and with every decision you make. Here are various techniques based on behavioural and action-based change which can be made part of your routine for long-lasting effect.

Behavioural activation

Behavioural activation is a technique that capitalises on the relationship between what you do and how you feel.[2] The theory behind it is simple: engaging in activity increases the opportunity to feel joy and therefore improves mood. You may already notice this in your daily life – for example, feeling calmer after taking a walk at lunchtime or feeling happier when seeing friends.

Specific types of activity can elicit different positive

responses. For example, engaging in things you enjoy, such as your hobbies, can give you feelings of pleasure. Spending time developing your skills or being challenged provides a sense of achievement and mastery which may lead to increased self-confidence and self-esteem. Spending time with other people and building positive healthy relationships can improve your wellbeing by encouraging you to feel valued and connected with others. So, when thinking about self-care, it is useful to reflect on how you spend your time and what you do to enjoy this time.

If there is no opportunity at work to socialise or meet colleagues, you may feel disconnected and isolated. However, if you make a conscious effort to connect with colleagues, this can increase a sense of belonging and bring fulfilment. The same argument can be made for including hobbies or exercise as part of self-care. These activities provide an opportunity for stress relief and achievement, both of which contribute to improved wellbeing. Engaging in behavioural activation will also create a positive maintenance cycle in which the more pleasurable the activity you engage in, the better your mood and wellbeing will be. This in turn will encourage you to continue engaging in activity, reinforcing the positive cycle (see Figure 12).

Purposefully engaging in activities as an act of self-care anchors you in the moment. Being involved, active and absorbed in something specific diverts you naturally away from distress. Individuals will have personal preferences for which behaviours contribute to their active practice of self-care. For example, many people enjoy participating in a sport, whereas others prefer to work creatively (e.g. drawing or painting) or engaging in a routine type of activity that requires focus and method (knitting or cooking). In developing your self-care practice, it is important to allow yourself the time and space to discover which activities work best for you. Activities that give you a

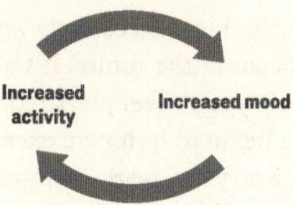

Figure 12: **A positive cycle triggered by behavioural activation**

sense of accomplishment, a sense of pride, connection and self-recognition, while absorbing you for a time, are usually the most effective sources of behavioural activation.

Self-care soothing

In addition, or as an alternative to active self-care behaviours, you might embrace soothing self-care practices. These are tools or activities that can be used to provide a sense of warmth and validation when in distress. For example, if you are prone to rumination for long periods of time – if you spend an excessive amount of time replaying an event in your mind or thinking about something that evokes negative emotions such as regret, bitterness or sadness – this will have a negative impact on your wellbeing. In this case, you could try the practice of *worry time,* first introduced by Borkovec et al. in 1983.[3]

Worry time is exactly what it sounds like. This time to worry, however, is strictly limited and bounded. The aim of worry time is to limit the overall amount of time spent worrying and thinking about things that are out of our control during a typical day. This is achieved by purposefully scheduling a time to worry. That may sound counter-intuitive, but has proved successful when used and recommended by counselling and clinical psychologists to support their patients.

Worry involves thinking excessively and negatively about events that could occur in the future. It's a normal feeling and in low doses can help you to feel prepared, safe and protected. However, when you begin to ruminate excessively or about lots of different topics, worry can begin to interfere with your daily living and mood, and will increase levels of anxiety. By learning to schedule in worry time you can begin to take control of rumination: by purposely focusing on worry, you become the master of your fears. You begin to dictate when you worry about something, rather than suffer constant unforeseen intrusions throughout your day.

The four steps to achieve worry time are outlined below. Although described from the perspective of an individual, worry time can also be modified to be used in teams. The concept of "worry time office hours" at the end of the working day might sound a little crazy but could go a long way to tackling worry and anxiety in a team or group. These office hours could encourage people either to work through their worries individually or to create a shared worry time to communicate team-specific fears.

1. **Create a worry time**. Make sure this lasts no more than 15 minutes during the day. It is important that the worry time occurs at the same time and place each day, but not in a place associated with rest or shortly before you are getting ready to sleep. Give yourself the appropriate amount of time to relax and unwind after the worry time. In the workplace, the objective is to clear out your mental fog by exposing your sources of worry to colleagues, and then thinking them through.

2. **Postpone your worries**. During the day, when a worry pops up, immediately make a note of it (on your phone, a Post-it

note, your diary) and remind yourself that you will come back to this worry at your dedicated worry time. Once you have postponed the worry, try to connect with the present moment. This could be by using mindfulness (see below) or by engaging in an activity to shift your attention (see the section on self-care behaviours earlier in this chapter).

3. **Engage in worry time.** At the prearranged time, spend time reflecting on the worries you noted down during the day (but only if they are still bothering you). It is also useful to write down your thoughts as opposed to worrying in your head. Taking each worry in turn, write out the worry, the source of concerns and its associated consequences and fears. Here you are giving yourself consent to worry as much as possible, with the aim of exhausting the worry and gaining a sense of control over when and how you ruminate. Return to worries in this time as often as you need, thereby, over time, reducing the intrusive nature of unannounced worries throughout the day.

4. **After-care.** Once your worry time is finished (after the 15-minute time limit), focus your attention on something else (not another worry or stress). This can be a relaxing activity or connecting with another person or pet. If worry time is completed at the end of the working day, it can be useful to focus on the rest of your evening or use your commute to move from the worry time to your evening.

Worry time works, but it might not be enough to help cope with sudden, difficult situations. In fact, when you are in high distress, it can sometimes be difficult to focus your attention or thoughts or have the energy to engage in activities that may improve your mood. When this happens, you can use other soothing practices, described below, to aid emotional distress and provide a sense of calm that can stabilise your mood until you are ready to engage in more active self-care methods.

Wellbeing and self-care tools

When in high distress, other wellbeing and self-care practices can help you cope with difficult emotions and foster positive wellbeing. When reading this section, it can be useful to reflect on how you relax or de-stress. Are there activities that help you relax and switch off after work? Or do you find it difficult to disconnect?

Mindfulness

Many of you will already be familiar with mindfulness. Mindfulness can include guided mediation, visual imagery and grounding exercises. To the surprise of many, the effect of mindfulness and meditation has been proved to have a range of positive outcomes at work. In fact, it has been a hot topic of research for almost two decades.[4] Evidence suggests, for example, that mindful practices can lower blood pressure and reduce fears and anxieties, and has been put to good use in professions prone to stress, such as nursing.[5]

Mindfulness grounds individuals in the present moment, and protects them against the impact that fear can have on their self-esteem. It is the conscious focus of attention without judgement on the self and on the present.

When practising mindfulness, you are aware of your current thoughts and feelings, but you do not dwell on or follow the sensations. Mindfulness is usually achieved through a conscious and active effort to focus on your breathing and return to the breath, whatever thoughts come to disrupt this focus. A common analogy is to think of yourself standing by the side of a road and watching cars pass. You are aware of the cars and may wave to the drivers as they pass, but you do not get into a car and follow them down the road. You also do not judge the cars: that car is driving too fast or slowly, this one is a horrible shade of green, or I like this car. The same is said for your thoughts: you acknowledge their presence neutrally but let them pass without judgement.

A simple routine for meditation at work could start by taking a break and finding a space in which you won't be disturbed: at your desk, or outside, in a nearby park, on a bench. Close your eyes and focus all your attention on breathing in and breathing out. Notice the sensation of your chest rising and falling. You could also consider counting to four for each inhalation and six for each exhalation. Your mind will start wandering to the latest email you need to address, or something that you have forgotten on your to-do list. Bring back your focus to your breath without self-judgement. Five minutes of such exercise might make a significant difference to your day. You can adjust the techniques and the environment, depending on what works best for you.

Visual imagery or guided imagery

This is a relaxation technique in which your imagination is used to picture a place, time or person that makes you feel peaceful, calm and happy. The imagery will be unique to you, as the aim is to create an image that you are emotionally drawn to. When using imagery, it is beneficial to involve as many of your senses as possible to interact with your image. For example, imagine you are walking on a hilly island filled with pine trees. What sounds can you hear? A bird singing, the wind in the trees? Can you smell the sea or the pine? Can your body feel the heat of the sun or the cool shade of the forest? The goal is to become fully immersed in your image to allow yourself a moment of relaxation for as long as you need.

Grounding

To go one step further, you could also consider using grounding exercises. These are used to connect yourself to the present and can be particularly helpful when you feel overwhelmed with emotion, disconnected from your environment, or when you are experiencing negative thoughts or distressing memories or feelings. When using grounding exercises, the goal is not to banish all distress but rather to create moments of peace and calm that will allow you to face your challenges feeling stronger and more resilient. Grounding is particularly helpful when feeling overwhelmed and in urgent need of peace.

A common grounding exercise is the five senses exercise.

1. Look around and name five things you can see. Describe them. What colour are they? Where are they placed?
2. Notice four things that you can feel. These could be an object you pick up or hold, the way your chair supports your back, or your feet on the floor.
3. Name three things you can hear. It can be helpful to close your eyes and take a moment to pick out the sounds around you. Can you hear birds? Or traffic in the street?
4. Notice two things you can smell. You can notice them in your surroundings or clothes. Can you smell your perfume or laundry detergent?
5. Take a moment to focus on one thing that you can taste. Can you still taste the coffee you drank this morning? Or your toothpaste?

This exercise is useful when you are feeling highly anxious. It can also be completed discreetly (instead of naming what you see orally, you can subtly notice these non-verbally). So this technique can even be used in team meetings or around others as often as needed. Your colleagues might see you mumbling but not much more than that. Before a stressful work task or event like a presentation, and as you fear you are losing your composure and cool, a grounding exercise might help you take a step away from the anxiety and regain control of yourself.

Journalling and gratitude

A final practice we recommend is based on another daily routine. The routine aspect is similar to the idea of worry time but the scope is much more significant: it is *journalling*. Like many, you might have found solace in journalling in your teenage years. But many of us lose the habit as we grow older. Journalling as a self-care act involves writing down (or doodling) your thoughts, feelings and events on a regular basis – possibly every day or every few days. It helps you to process experiences in all areas of your life and builds greater self-awareness.

The habit of journalling can help you to become more conscious of your thoughts and feelings and can be especially useful for anyone who may struggle to articulate their feelings verbally or with others. People may feel psychologically safer writing down their emotions and reflections than sharing them with a supportive other. Journalling provides a literal space to explore and uncover your inner world without the expectations or assumptions of other people. When journalling is done with openness and honesty, it can be a vital tool for wellbeing. It helps put negative experience and emotions on paper, and to leave them behind.

Gratitude can also soothe distress. Research has demonstrated that those who practise gratitude daily report an increased general sense of wellbeing and decreased stress hormones.[6] Gratitude practices include listing and reflecting on things, people and experiences you are grateful for. At work, it's easy to focus only on aspects of your jobs that are a source of fear and anxiety. Using gratitude, you can begin to focus on the parts of work that you appreciate, increasing your positive feelings associated to the workplace. For example: I am grateful for my friendly colleague; I am grateful for the opportunity to demonstrate my problem-solving skills; I am grateful for my morning coffee break; I am grateful for the support I can provide to clients or patients; I am grateful to be excited by what I do.

Beyond self-care

Self-care is an important practice to support and strengthen wellbeing. However, there may be times when you need to supplement self-care or when the support of others and professional help is needed. There are limits and potential dangers to relying on self-assessment and self-care only: blind spots and biases can mean you do not get an accurate sense of your wellbeing. For example, a people pleaser who is unfamiliar with considering their needs may assume that things are all right and they are coping fine. Alternatively, even if someone's wellbeing is poor, they may be in denial and tell themselves that they can cope because not coping would feel too dangerous and overwhelming. Therefore, it is useful to recognise and understand when an outside perspective is needed. In the same way that you might ask for feedback on your work, you may need feedback and support on your wellbeing. The checklist opposite is a useful first step for identifying when to seek further support from your organisation or a qualified professional.

CHECKLIST 4 **When is further support needed?**

· There has been no change or improvement in mood (as assessed using questionnaires).

· I cannot understand or map out my feelings (using the hot cross bun model).

· I feel stuck in a maintenance cycle.

· I am struggling to recognise my thoughts or struggling to challenge my thoughts.

· I have difficulty with taking perspective.

· Worry time is making me feel even more worried.

· I am no longer interested in connecting with others and am isolating myself.

· Enjoyable usual activities are not feeling pleasurable.

· I am struggling to relax despite engaging with soothing practices.

· I feel at risk or my personal safety is compromised.

· I want to discuss my wellbeing with others. **(You do not need to wait until your wellbeing deteriorates to ask for help.)**

All the tools described in Part 2, from the questionnaires and an understanding of maintenance cycles to mindfulness, grounding and journalling techniques, are proactive ways to care for yourself. They are not silver bullets, but they are simple tools you may want to try until you feel comfortable with one, two or several of them. They are all proved to contribute to a healthier routine. An anxious worker may decide to start mindfulness and journalling every day after or before work. But when they see themselves stuck in a spiral of negative thinking, they may want to go back to the list of cognitive distortions to understand where they stand and how they can challenge themselves. Wellbeing intelligence starts in this first circle – with the self – and is about developing the right habits for you and your own context.

These techniques can be shared with others, as well as using them yourself. Remember, though, that your ability to support other people with these practices of self-care – getting others to use these practices or guiding them to do so – depends on how comfortable you are with these practices yourself. In the next part of the book, we will build on this to apply similar techniques when supporting others and to look at approaches designed for team and one-to-one assistance.

PART 3

The second circle of wellbeing intelligence: supporting teams and co-workers

Elias was having the monthly catch-up with his intern, Mustapha. Mustapha had been an incredible member of the team so far, but in the last couple of months, he seemed anxious and stressed when they met. Mustapha was making stupid mistakes and was losing his composure in meetings. Elias was starting to think that Mustapha was not as good as he had initially thought, but suspected that more was at play. But how should Elias open that conversation? His relationship with Mustapha so far had been very formal and professional – just like the culture of the company.

Elias finally found the right words to ask Mustapha about the cause of his anxiety. Mustapha admitted reluctantly to some personal struggles: his mother was in a poor state of health, and he had to step up to support her and his family, which was preventing him from fully engaging with work. As he struggled to give his attention to his job, he was feeling increasingly stressed. He was concerned that he might be perceived as a poor performer and slacker.

Elias was left speechless. He had never faced such a situation, as he always felt conditioned to remain guarded and not discuss personal issues at work. But he believes Mustapha has huge potential and wants to help him.

This central section of the book focuses on how individuals can help those around them: their collaborators, their team members, their boss. Importantly, the first chapter starts by exploring the potential causes of people's wellbeing difficulties at work – whether they are about the relationships with their colleagues, or the challenges related to working practices within the organisation. The tools explored in Part 1 are then reconsidered and applied to assess the mental health of others.

6

Detecting mental health difficulties in others

Heather and Graham work in the IT department of a large national energy company. They work well together and have a friendly relationship, often sharing jokes over coffee. One morning, Heather arrived early to find Graham already at work, staring blankly at his computer screen, his coffee untouched and growing cold. Heather found this concerning, and straightaway felt something was off.

Over the next few days Heather noticed Graham was not his usual self. Typically, Graham thrives on collaboration and takes pleasure in joining the rest of the team for lunch, but lately he has been withdrawn and isolated. Heather decided to reach out to Graham and ask him if everything was all right. Initially reluctant to talk, Graham then shared how he had been feeling, his racing thoughts, increased anxiety and difficulty sleeping. He has been unreasonably worried about financial difficulties and in particular repaying his student loan. Heather, by simply surfacing the source of his anxiety, helped Graham process this situation and realise it was not all as bad as he thought: objectively, he would be able to go through repayment with a bit of additional care with his spending. She encouraged Graham to seek professional support and talk to his doctor, and, in the meantime, suggested they use their regular coffee meetings to check in so Graham remembered he was not alone.

The aim of this chapter is to encourage the detection of poor wellbeing within the workplace, and give it visibility, without shame, as Heather was able to do with Graham. We explore the weight of stigma on mental ill health, and describe the common risk factors that managers and colleagues can look out for when identifying poor wellbeing in others. We then offer some practical tools to aid assessment and begin to normalise a culture of wellbeing at work.

Overcoming stigma

For many people, disclosing the state of their wellbeing can feel very uncomfortable. This can be especially true in the workplace or with colleagues, where professionalism is prioritised. Many fear the stigma associated with not coping and will worry about the potential negative perceptions of others (and themselves). The real or perceived stigma associated with poor mental health can be detrimental to wellbeing. Stigma can silence individuals, leaving them isolated and alone. Because of this silence, individuals suffering from mental health tend to think they are alone. Stigma can also prevent people from accessing timely and appropriate support, which often increases feelings of self-doubt. Poor wellbeing is then exacerbated.

Although there is increasingly more disclosure of poor mental health at work, people are still reluctant to share their troubles and are more likely to present themselves as being well because of the fear of stigma or being seen as not coping.[1] Many fear the possible consequences of disclosure, such as limited career progression opportunity, lack of consideration, reduced responsibility and, in some cases, a change of identity.

Think about the example of Carrie. Carrie returned from

long-term sick leave due to stress-induced stomach ulcers. After recovering physically, she was feeling ready and capable to return to work, though admittedly a bit apprehensive. When she returned to her job, her line manager took the time to ensure that Carrie was up to date with everything she needed to know and offered a gradual return. Initially Carrie found this helpful and was feeling confident in her work. However, she noticed her nervousness when colleagues asked how she was and why she went off sick. She was also embarrassed by new members of the team who had been told about her sick leave and had been covering for her while she was away. Carrie found these questions began to shake her confidence, so she decided to overcompensate and return to work full time, while making a conscious effort to present herself as assertive and self-possessed.

Deep down Carrie was feeling overwhelmed and anxious; she could feel her stress levels rising and was worried about her health. However, she was unwilling to share this with her line manager as she didn't want to go back on sick leave or reduce her hours. She felt others would think she was no longer able to do her job, and she would be regarded poorly by the rest of the team. Instead, she continued to act as though she was fine, trapping herself in a vicious maintenance cycle due to fear of stigma, and potentially putting her health at risk.

Fears of stigma can be justified and part of a manager's role is to act as a good role model when discussing wellbeing. This may mean managers share how they feel – for example: "I feel energised after our brainstorming session" or "I feel tired after our department meeting, because there was so much content to cover." Though sounding rather casual or superficial, small interactions and comments such as these can begin to normalise sharing and give unconscious permission for others to share too. Managers can also reduce fears around stigma by being mindful of the language used to describe poor wellbeing – for example, avoiding flippant and dismissive terms such as "insane", "grumpy", "man up" or "time of the month". In Chapter 9, we will look in more detail at issues around vocabulary and culture.

Managers and leaders can also validate the emotions and the experience of others. For example, if someone has had to deal with a difficult customer, a manager can validate how they might be feeling and show their understanding by recognising that they may feel more sensitive to criticism or upset after the exchange. In most cases, they will have experienced similar feelings earlier in their career. Having a trusted manager who can offer a positive response to disclosure not only takes away the stigma; it also increases feelings of self-acceptance and aids recovery.[2]

Risk factors to poor wellbeing in the workplace

Mental health difficulties can easily be hidden; many people are good at *masking* their symptoms and experience. This may be due to not wanting to share their difficulties or because they do not feel that it is acceptable or wanted by others. It can be hard to determine when someone is in distress if there are no visual signals or sharing. Therefore, the expectation on managers is not to become mind-readers but rather to acknowledge that they may not always have the full picture when it comes to the workings of their colleagues' mental health.

Some wellbeing difficulties may be invisible, especially when they do not fit neatly into the diagnostic categories or symptoms described in Chapter 2. So it is important to be aware of potential risk factors to wellbeing in the workplace. This means that even when colleagues are not directly expressing their distress, you can still check in and be available for others when they would like to share. Here are some common manifestations and signs of likely wellbeing issues to look out for at work

Isolation

When people who are usually sociable begin to isolate themselves from colleagues, they are sending a fundamental clue. For some people, having lunch alone is their preference and norm. They may get overstimulated by others or prefer to take some time away from work, and this supports their wellbeing. However, if you notice someone who usually joins the team for lunch suddenly becoming distant, this may indicate a change in mood and prompt a conversation about their current experience.

Nikos, a valuable colleague, was quieter than usual and would mostly fake laughter at office jokes after some hesitation. He was distancing himself during lunchtimes and often leaving the office or staff room when others entered. Perhaps Nikos was just no longer enjoying spending time with his colleagues, or was disengaged. But the simple effort of asking him how he is doing and suggesting that his change of behaviour is a source of concern might help him to open up about his personal situation. In fact, Nikos has just ended a committed long-term relationship. He and his partner have been separated for months and after reflection and space decided to end the relationship. Nikos has not shared his home situation with anyone at work. They all knew him as the fun-loving, jokey guy who was quick to smile and crack a joke. However, since his relationship ended, he has been feeling increasingly depressed and struggling to connect at work. Simply starting a conversation with Nikos may help him to share his current difficulties. This does not need to be a full-blown conversation in which intimate details are shared, but people should have the room to display vulnerability. This would show Nikos that he is supported at work and help him to rebuild his connections with others.

Bullying

Workplace bullying can come from difficult work relationships, team dynamics and organisational culture. Some bullying may be obvious and direct. This could involve harmful words and behaviours, consistently criticising work performance, or badmouthing others and spreading rumours. Other times, bullying can be indirect and subtle – for example, deliberately giving an individual a higher workload than others, or purposely excluding someone from a workplace chat group.

Workplace bullying can occur between colleagues, and across the manager–employee relationship, in either direction. Subordinate or upwards bullying can occur when an employee intentionally acts to undermine and disrespect their manager. Bullying of any kind can have a negative impact on an individual's wellbeing and their team.

Greta was an experienced accountant who had recently moved into a management position at a new company. Although new to managing people, Greta had prepared by attending training and building on her experience of process management. In her new position, Greta would be line managing Sara, an experienced bookkeeper, who had been at the company for almost 15 years. Though initially welcoming to Greta, Sara quickly became cold and critical of Greta's work. Greta was keen to update processes in line with recommended practice but found she would be faced with resistance. Sara claimed that "this is how it's always worked" and refused to try any new practices, while complaining to others that Greta didn't know enough about how the company works. As this continued, Greta began to doubt her ability as a manager, and was left feeling unconfident in her new role and unwelcome in the company. Greta also began to dread her meetings with Sara as their interactions were filled with tension.

It's easy to think that a more senior person can handle bullying by themselves. But it is important to recognise the signs of *any* colleagues being bullied. Often, bullies will enjoy the presence of witnesses, which makes the bullying process public.

Workload (actual and cognitive)

Understanding the relationship between workload and mood is useful for recognising patterns of wellbeing. You can expect to see a peak in stress and anxiety as workload increases. Though this is a typical and expected response, it is wise to acknowledge and, if necessary, monitor the stress to ensure that poor wellbeing does not become a constant state. Also consider that the *actual* workload of tasks to complete, meetings to attend or reports to write may differ from the *cognitive* workload experienced. For example, thoughts about how competent someone feels about completing tasks will influence how much energy is thought to be needed in succeeding. If meetings involve working with uncooperative partners, the mental workload will be higher than when working with amicable and amenable colleagues.

Colleagues have been worried about Maribelle, a recently qualified teacher, who returned to the classroom at the start of the school year. Maribelle understood and expected that her workload would be very heavy during the school terms, but assumed that over the school holidays she would have some respite and a lower workload. Although this was the case, she found her cognitive load was higher at the times when her actual workload was low. Although she spent some of her school breaks planning her upcoming lessons, she found that most of her time was spent worrying about how busy the next term would be, and how little time she would have for herself once school began. With the new term approaching, Maribelle's anticipatory anxiety was so great that she was unable to enjoy her time off and recharge during the school break. Her colleagues found her to be exhausted at her return; they were puzzled to find someone tired after the school holidays. But without her colleagues stepping in to support her, Maribelle will be at greater risk of burnout, because her cognitive workload has compromised her ability to fulfil her actual workload.

Job (in)security

In times of company hardship, corporate change or uncertainty, people may find it difficult to relax into their roles. Job security is key to wellbeing at work; stable employment leading to financial stability can reduce one of the biggest stressors experienced by adults. Without job security, it is common for fear to spread across teams. People will struggle to engage and be productive in their jobs, as they wait for news about their futures. Managers may also notice an increase in questions from employees and find they will have to offer reassurance and seek further information on their behalf. Managers may feel insecure about their own jobs and have to contain these fears as they try to allay their teams' worry.

Job insecurity is rife for those with zero-hours contracts. The highly unpredictable work pattern (and often low pay) are triggers for stress, anxiety and chronic worry – consequences that need to be taken seriously.

Philip, a restaurant owner, has hired Iain, a young and energetic individual who recently graduated from university. The job is on a zero-hours contract, which means that he will work only when needed, and his hours could vary greatly from week to week. At first, Philip found Iain was excited about the flexibility as he acknowledged it would give him time to apply for graduate schemes and spend time with his friends. However, as time went on, the reality of a zero-hours contract began to set in. Some weeks, Iain would work almost every day, leaving him exhausted and with little time for anything else. Other weeks, he would work very few hours, which made it difficult for him to plan his finances or potential interviews for other jobs. The unpredictability of his schedule also made it hard to maintain a healthy lifestyle. Philip realised that Iain ate at irregular times and would skip meals because of his varying work hours. Iain revealed that he felt isolated, as his changing schedule made it difficult to make and keep plans with friends. It was clear that Iain had also struggled to form relationships with his colleagues, because of his varying shifts. Philip soon realised that the way he was managing the workload for Iain was taking a toll on Iain's wellbeing, and decided to offer him a more stable set of hours that could help him balance work and life better.

Survivor's guilt

Managers should expect survivor's guilt after a particularly tricky organisational shift – for example, after mass redundancies or a change of senior management. Morale is likely to be low across the team, and members may directly question why they survived and kept their job while others did not. Managers may also notice that employees may try to prove their worth, and demonstrate that that are worthy of staying. Survivor's guilt may follow or precede periods of job insecurity within a company, and will be particularly present in those with high levels of empathy or where teams work very closely together.

Olive was a dedicated project manager working for a tech

start-up. She was professional and capable and known for her commitment and ability to bring out the best in her team members. However, due to the covid pandemic, the managers of the start-up had to make the difficult decision to downsize. Several of Olive's colleagues, some of whom she had worked with since the company's launch, were laid off. Olive and others were kept on, but the aftermath was challenging. She found her team members, and to some extent herself, grappling with survivor's guilt. Her employees told her explicitly they felt guilty for still having a job while their colleagues, equally deserving and hardworking, were let go. The team's productivity began to suffer, and Olive knew that many of her team members were wondering if they could be next. The office seemed emptier, the workload heavier, and the atmosphere more tense. Olive knew that something needed to change to protect her team's wellbeing.

Imposter syndrome

Imposter syndrome is defined as an internal experience of self-doubt and lack of self-belief despite genuine achievements and success. It can be tricky to spot because, most of the time, individuals with imposter syndrome will be hard working, conscientious and eager to please. However, imposter syndrome is very common, and it is likely that everyone will experience it at some stage in their career.

People with imposter syndrome are likely to experience low self-esteem, and will often dismiss and minimise their achievements, attributing their performance to luck, which diminishes their achievements. Imposter syndrome can be identified by negative self-talk and a reluctance to celebrate and acknowledge their good work. People might also show greater checking behaviours or seek reassurance as their belief in their own ability changes. People with imposter syndrome are less likely to volunteer for tasks or take the lead. They may also not speak out in meetings or brainstorming sessions for fear of being wrong or "caught out".

Imposter syndrome is usually present in people who are new in their role or newly qualified. It may also be present in those who have returned to work after a career break. However, as an individual becomes familiar with their new role and workplace, one would expect their confidence to grow and feelings of imposter syndrome to lessen. Therefore, it's important to be mindful of the wellbeing of new starters.

Longer-term instances of imposter syndrome may indicate a more general lack of confidence or self-esteem. These people may also be anxious about receiving feedback on their work because of a fear of being "found out" or, alternatively, they might frequently justify their work to others to prove they know what they are doing. In this case, you need to be specific and clear in your praise. A generic "Well done" may not be believed by someone experiencing imposter syndrome; most likely they will feel you are just saying this because you should or it's expected. Specific feedback and praise demonstrate to the employee that their work has been valued and that they bring value, knowledge and skills to the team.

Lucas, a newly qualified physiotherapist, is joining a multidisciplinary team at his local hospital. Before training, he gained many years of work experience and performed very well in his studies. Lucas is joining a team with a range of professionals with various experiences and qualifications. But despite his qualifications and achievements, he often found himself doubting his abilities. He felt like a fraud among his experienced colleagues and feared that one day, they would discover he wasn't as competent as they thought. Lucas would spend extra hours at work, double-checking patient notes and preparing for case meetings. Despite receiving positive feedback from peers and patients, he attributed his success to luck rather than to his abilities.

Tools to detect wellbeing in others

Conversations about wellbeing are useful to understand and detect someone's state of wellbeing. However, not everyone will be willing to engage in intimate or direct conversations. Therefore, light-touch tools can encourage others to share but also provide opportunities for noticing wellbeing in a neutral, casual manner.

Check-ins and check-outs

In team meetings, managers can give themselves and the team dedicated time to check in and share how they are currently feeling, a work-related achievement, or something they are looking forward to. Dedicating specific time in team meetings for a wellbeing check demonstrates to all employees that wellbeing is important and everyone can contribute positively to how others are feeling. Similarly, check-outs can be used to give the team a space to reflect on how meetings have gone and if everyone feel satisfied or clear about the outcomes.

It's important to take note of how colleagues engage with this task. If a team member struggles to think of anything positive, this may indicate that their wellbeing is poor or that their self-care is being neglected. Similarly, if someone struggles to think of something they are proud of, it may indicate that they are not feeling fulfilled or proud of their work.

Non-work sharing

Creating spaces during the working day to make time for colleagues to discuss things not connected to work is useful to build deeper connections. Non-work sharing also acts as a gentle reminder to reflect on life outside work, illustrating a healthy work–life balance. Non-work sharing can be varied and may include time on Monday mornings to talk about the weekend; keeping a note of people's birthdays, or asking about holiday experiences. What you learn from these encounters is not only an indication of an individual's wellbeing, but also their work–life balance. The level of non-work sharing will also reveal how comfortable people feel sharing with each other, and ultimately their capacity for supporting others.

Wellbeing agendas

In weekly or monthly one-to-one meetings and annual reviews, wellbeing can formally be added to the agenda, and managers can make a point of asking about people's experiences. Taking this more holistic approach shows that colleagues are seen not just as workers, but as whole people. Wellbeing agendas formalise wellbeing as part of an individual's experience at work, and can examine the relationship between work and wellbeing. They also provide an opportunity to evaluate work through the lens of wellbeing and for either party to comment on and evaluate how the working environment, context and job roles affect wellbeing. This could also be an opportunity to discuss any company-wide support or initiatives that may be necessary or useful to encourage wellbeing.

With all these tools, the aim is to encourage sharing and to support others' wellbeing without stigma or shame. It is also important to recognise that wellbeing can be fluid: if someone checks in feeling a particular way one day, they may not feel the same the next day or week. Engagement with non-work sharing may also vary, but regular check-ins and wellbeing agendas will normalise and validate conversations about mental health. They make it possible to take the pulse of people in a way that does not feel awkward or unnatural.

Assessing mental health risks in others

Part of detecting and supporting wellbeing with others will involve, at times and in the most difficult scenarios, an assessment of psychological risk and personal safety. Understanding an individual's level of risk will mean that managers are in a prime position to signpost to the most appropriate support as soon as necessary. Managers are not expected to hold the risk, but if someone shares information that may put them or others in harm's way, everyone has a duty of care to act on the information.

Assessing risk will involve assessing for suicidal thoughts, plans and intentions to self-harm. Although asking about suicide can feel daunting and at times uncomfortable, it can be crucial when the risk has clearly emerged. The ask suicide-screening questions (ASQ) toolkit is a useful tool to support assessing risk in such drastic situation.[3] This is a set of four yes/no suicide-screening questions, designed to take only 20 seconds to go through (see Table 6). The ASQ aims to give a quick assessment of current risk and can be used by all.

Assessing risk in this level of detail may feel unfamiliar and scary. Therefore, we encourage managers and peers to be led by the individual sharing the information. This is not expected to be a routine conversation, but only used when someone shares distressing thoughts of hurting themselves or indicates self-harm. There is also no expectation for others to solve these problems; the expectation is to refer them to appropriate professional support.

TABLE 6 **The ask suicide-screening questions (ASQ) tool**

1. In the past few weeks, have you wished you were dead?	Yes/No
2. In the past few weeks, have you felt that you or your family would be better off if you were dead?	Yes/No
3. In the past week, have you been having thoughts about killing yourself?	Yes/No
4. Have you ever tried to kill yourself? If yes, how? When?	Yes/No
If the respondent answers "Yes" to any of the above questions, ask the following acuity question: 5. Are you having thoughts of killing yourself right now? If yes, please describe.	Yes/No
If the respondent answers "Yes" to question 5, managers should immediately help the individual to get in touch with the emergency support services for a full mental health evaluation and subsequent monitoring and treatment.	

Confidentiality

When holding wellbeing conversations, the listener is trusted with the information shared. Such conversation will contain private details, experiences and personal history. These sensitive details must be kept confidential and must not be passed on to other people. However, there will be limitations to this confidentiality. In certain circumstances, information (including personal details) will have to be shared with others, either within the organisation or externally. Therefore it is imperative that organisations have a confidentiality agreement in place to outline explicitly the ways in which sensitive information, once disclosed, will be treated, and the conditions under which information may be shared.

Confidentially agreements do not have to be overly long and detailed. A clear statement that is included alongside other company policies is sufficient. For example:

As an organisation that cares about wellbeing, you may find yourself engaged in conversations about mental health and wellbeing. These interactions will likely involve the sharing of sensitive information. As part of the organisation's confidentiality policy, all sensitive information and private details must be kept confidential and not shared with any other third party. However, there may be circumstances where information must be shared to prevent further harm to self or others, or to access appropriate support. Typically, information will be shared in the following cases.

1. When the individual sharing has given consent for confidentiality to be broken and information shared in a selected way. This may be to assist a referral to HR or Occupational Health to implement necessary workplace changes or an external wellbeing organisation for timely and appropriate treatment.

2. When the information shared is of such gravity that confidentiality cannot be maintained. This includes instances in which the listener considers the individual or others to be at risk of harm or imminent danger. In these situations, there is a duty of care to share required information.

A robust confidentiality agreement can create trust and confidence in wellbeing conversations, and both the listener and the sharer can feel safe in the knowledge that shared details will be respected and handled appropriately. Knowing the extent of confidentiality can foster trust in relationships and reassure those who share that their privacy is valued.

Early intervention and recognising unhealthy coping

Workplaces, colleagues and managers are not expected to act as, or to replace, healthcare organisations and professionals. However, acknowledging mental health distress in the workplace can be hugely important in supporting an individual's overall wellbeing.

Every interaction at work has the potential to have an impact on wellbeing. For some, a wellbeing conversation or team check-in could be the first step in someone's wellbeing journey. Bringing wellbeing into work can support others to understand and reflect on their wellbeing and mental state, and help them on to the path of support and recovery. These interactions are vital as each connection has the potential to change a life for the better. Therefore the ways in which people relate and connect with others at work can act as a prompt for early intervention – either by using the tools outlined in Part 2 or here in Part 3 to help a colleague cope with their mental health issues, or by encouraging and supporting someone to seek professional help in more complex cases.

Early intervention is crucial in preventing a severe mental health crisis. Understanding the risk factors to poor wellbeing at work and using tools to encourage sharing are all methods to encourage an individual to access timely and appropriate support. Early detection can protect against deterioration of mood and also reduce the isolation and stigma typically associated with poor wellbeing.

Early intervention can normalise sharing so that those in distress do not have to cope alone or suffer in silence. It also encourages greater participation and engagement with treatment services that promote recovery and build resilience for future poor wellbeing episodes, all of which will have an indirectly positive influence on how someone relates to their work and organisation.

Learning to detect poor wellbeing in others may uncover and support those who are struggling to cope. Early detection can benefit an entire team. It is likely that teams will share specific workplace stressors, perhaps a lack of clarity with deadlines, or unpredictable working patterns. So when this is recognised in one member of the team, it may help everyone else. Responding to early detection and supporting those with wellbeing difficulties can also create positive role modelling. Witnessing a colleague or manager being open and discussing wellbeing (generally or specifically) can encourage others to reflect and share their wellbeing concerns. And when key stressors are identified and known, managers can use this information to pre-empt potential distress and protect team wellbeing in the future.

Early detection and intervention also promotes more healthy coping strategies. Without support, individuals may turn to coping mechanisms that involve detrimental behaviours, such as excessive alcohol consumption, substance use, self-harm or emotional eating. Understandably, the aim of these unhelpful strategies is to manage the immediate distress regardless of any long-term consequences. However, overreliance on unhelpful coping strategies will perpetuate poor wellbeing. In some cases, identifying unhelpful coping mechanisms may point to underlying distress, which can then be addressed.

The ability to detect mental health issues among employees is a critical skill in today's workplace. It requires a keen understanding of the signs and symptoms of various mental health conditions outlined in Chapter 2, and also a more specific understanding of poor mental wellbeing and what causes it. Awareness is nothing without a delicate, compassionate and empathetic response.

With check-ins and check-outs, wellbeing agendas and

personal sharing, you can promote open dialogue about mental health, fostering a more supportive work environment where mental wellbeing can be discussed more openly. We will connect and develop these principles in Chapter 9 where we focus on the development of an organisational culture that builds on team support and encourages key strategies and polices at an organisational level.

7

Wellbeing tools to support others

Martina and Leona work together in a large company. They are part of a close-knit group of colleagues who joined the company as graduate trainees at the same time, and have developed a close friendship. Over time, Martina noticed a change in Leona's behaviour. Leona, usually cheerful and energetic, seemed withdrawn and less enthusiastic about work. Her performance started to decline, and she often looked tired and stressed. Martina, being concerned, decided to address the issue and invited Leona for a cup of coffee.

As they sat in the quiet corner of the café, Martina gently broached the subject. "Leona, I've noticed you've been a bit off lately. Is everything okay?" Leona hesitated before finally opening up about the pressures she was facing both at work and home. She confessed that she was finding it hard to maintain a balance and was feeling overwhelmed with adapting to work from university. Martina listened attentively, offering words of comfort and understanding. She suggested that Leona might benefit from speaking to a professional counsellor provided by their company's health insurance. She also thanked Leona for sharing and told her that seeking help was a step towards regaining control. Leona was initially resistant, but Martina's non-judgemental approach and reassurance made her reconsider, and she agreed to explore the support options available.

In the following weeks, Leona started attending counselling sessions. Gradually, there was a noticeable improvement in her demeanour and performance at work. Leona thanked Martina for her timely coffee invitation and initial conversation. Just one conversation had given her a push to talk about her issues, and to seek the right help.

The value of a supportive team

This chapter reinforces the idea of wellbeing as a workstyle rather than a tick-box exercise. Wellbeing intelligence is not about checking in with wellbeing sporadically, but a shift in how wellbeing at work is perceived more generally. The approach involves the validation in the thinking, language and acknowledging of wellbeing in the workplace. Wellbeing is a holistic experience that cannot be switched off or dropped off at the door as someone walks into an office or sits at their desk. In this sense, wellbeing involves bringing your whole self to work. This means that aspects of the self and personality are not hidden when at work, and the self that is presented goes beyond a job title. Bringing the whole self to work can encompass personal style, culture, hobbies, sexuality, family circumstances, and current mood, physical and mental health.

This kind of honesty with oneself takes work, as shown by the example of Aaliyah, who joined as a software engineer at a tech company. This was her first full-time job and initially she had a hard time bringing her authentic self to work because she felt she didn't identify with other engineers. She enjoyed solving problems, creating great user experiences, supporting others, and a good team atmosphere. However, she felt that these aspects of her personality didn't align with the stereotypical image of an engineer. Over time, Aaliyah started to share these traits and found her perspective and skills were valuable and needed in her team. She started to express her ideas more openly and took the initiative to lead projects that focused on improving user experiences. She also began to support her colleagues more actively, offering help when they faced challenges. Aaliyah's whole self started to shine through in her work, and her colleagues appreciated her insights and the positive atmosphere she created in the team. She was able to bring all parts of herself to work and contribute her unique skills and perspectives.

The ability to bring the whole self to work means that people are not masking or dismissing parts of themselves, but rather being true to themselves and towards others. Although Aaliyah's story focuses on personality traits, being true to yourself can also involve a willingness to share your wellbeing state with others, and strengthen the support gained from others.

The connections and relationships made at work not only form part of our social circle but can also influence the way you think and feel about your job and career. For example, people with encouraging managers may feel confident about their career progression as they access mentors and opportunity. Equally, friendly colleagues who are willing to share their work practices can help newcomers settle in and feel competent in their roles. However, those with hostile and unwelcoming peers may feel isolated at work and then leave, creating a workplace with a high turnover. People with an unsympathetic manager who values work above all else may experience burnout in trying to meet impossibly high expectations.

Ultimately, there are many benefits of being a support to colleagues and having support from others at work. Supportive others provide emotional validation and acceptance in times of stress. They also help to build social connections, which means loneliness and isolation are reduced, even in times of great overwhelm. Colleagues can also be a source of inspiration when managing our wellbeing, offering ideas on how to cope, solve problems or move forward with stressors. On top of these wellbeing benefits, research demonstrates that good team connections can improve worker performance, reduce intra-group conflict and increase the likelihood for employees to go above and beyond their call of duty, behaving as citizens rather than in a transactional way.[1]

Psychological safety at work

Supportive others can cultivate an environment of psychological safety. Psychological safety is the absence of interpersonal fear when sharing thoughts and ideas. It is the principle that you will not be punished or humiliated for speaking up with ideas, questions, concerns or mistakes.[2] Individuals who feel psychologically safe can share ideas and thoughts without fear of judgement or reprimand. High psychological safety can create an environment that allows for both positive and negative feedback to be freely shared and accepted and lead to further improvements, learning and success. When individuals feel psychologically safe, they can perform at their best; within teams, high psychological safety improves effectiveness, employee retention and learning.[3]

Specifically, within workplaces, we can talk about *team psychological safety*.[4] This is a shared belief held by members of a group that it is acceptable to ask questions, share concerns and mistakes, and take risks without the fear of negative consequences from the group.

Positive peer relationships founded on respectful communication can increase feelings of familiarity between team members and leaders, which encourage psychological safety.[5] In teams with high turnover or lone working, direct communication and familiarity with peers can be reduced and psychological safety may also be found elsewhere, such as with mentors and role models who can normalise vulnerability and sharing.

Everyone has a role to play in creating psychologically safe work environments, but leaders and managers have a particular role by actively encouraging curiosity and questioning, and using inclusive language when discussing successes, challenges and explicitly asking for contributions. For example:

- What did we do well?
- What have we learnt from our recent project?

By encouraging contributions from others and appreciating and acknowledging when others share, people learn to engage more with fellow team members and take risks without shame or fear. Admitting mistakes also needs to be rewarded as part of the journey.

In a workplace, it's all too easy for the opposite of psychological safety to arise: *psychological danger*. Psychological danger develops when people do not trust each other, think that the reasons for mistakes are well known (the "common knowledge effect"), and do not want to admit when they are wrong. Psychological safety promotes mutual learning, and leads to cycles of performance: the team unpacks what is to be improved and continuously improve. When the team has performed poorly, the team members can take stock and examine their past practices to improve. By contrast, psychological danger will trigger a vicious cycle of poor performance leading to more distrust and even poorer performance. In this sense, psychological safety within the workplace is important for the growth and success of a team but will also have huge impact on wellbeing by helping people rebuild morale when performance has been low, and turn things around when needed.

The work of peers and leaders can be further reinforced by organisational procedures and practices that promote psychological safety. We will explore this more in Part 4.

Conversations about wellbeing

Effective communication, careful use of language and active listening can help to create a psychologically safe workplace. Although these skills can be used in all workplace interactions, they are particularly useful when discussing wellbeing difficulties. Once managers or peers are aware of risk factors to wellbeing or recognise when someone is struggling, the next step is to begin a supportive conversation.

For many, talking about wellbeing can feel intimidating or even intrusive, especially at work, where people want to be seen to be professional, and personal lives are *supposed* to remain personal. However, the ability to talk about wellbeing is key to becoming wellbeing intelligent. What follows are some models and steps to inspire productive and encouraging wellbeing conversations with others.

Core conditions

The core conditions, developed by psychologist Carl Rogers in the 1950s in the context of therapist–patient relationships, can act as a guide for how best to approach wellbeing conversations at work. Rogers proposed that there are six necessary and sufficient conditions required for "therapeutic change" to occur within a person.[6] Of the six conditions, three (empathy, congruence and unconditional positive regard) are referred to as the "core conditions", which can inform and enhance wellbeing conversations across many settings, including those beyond therapy.

Empathy

The first of the three core conditions is empathy. Empathy is defined as understanding from the other person's frame of reference. It involves attempting to understand the other person's perspective and is an active process of being and feeling with someone, working to truly understand their thoughts, feelings and experiences. Empathy goes beyond sympathy. When demonstrating empathy, the purpose is not to express sorrow or pity for someone's experience (feeling *for* someone) but rather compassionately understanding someone's experience (feeling *with* someone). Being empathic means that you want to understand the other person's experience, and even if you cannot fully understand or share the same experience, acknowledge that it is still valid to the person experiencing it. In this sense, empathy is not about problem solving or trying to fix things; the emphasis is on making the sharer feel heard. Empathy can also be expressed non-verbally in body language that is open and inviting.

Congruence

The next core condition is congruence. Congruence means that you, as the listener, are responding genuinely: you are being yourself, responding and interacting truthfully without playing a role. This works to build trust in your relationship with the other person, and in turn encourages sharing without fear of rejection or stigma. For managers and colleagues, this means they remain respectful and avoid any false promises or insincere sympathy. When acting congruently, there is an element of self-reflection, because being congruent means you become aware of your own thoughts and feelings in response to the other person. At times, this self-reflection might mean that you share your own thoughts and experiences when helpful.

Unconditional positive regard

The third core condition is unconditional positive regard (UPR). UPR is about being non-judgemental when listening to others. When offering UPR, you look to accept what is being shared with warmth, so that the other person feels valued. "Unconditional" does not mean that all behaviours are accepted; rather, that you are unconditional in your respect and warmth. It's a way of enabling others to share worries and distress without fear of judgement or rejection.

To see how the core conditions can be used in practice, let's go back to the story in Chapter 6 of Lucas, the physiotherapist who was experiencing imposter syndrome and constantly doubting himself. His colleague Manjula, also a physiotherapist, noticed he was spending a lot of time overpreparing for meetings. The next time Manjula and Lucas were on a shift together, she decided to ask him about how he was finding his new role. Lucas was grateful for her question and decided to open up to Manjula about how he was feeling.

- **Empathy.** Manjula listened attentively as Lucas shared his anxiety about work and insecurities within the team. Instead of offering advice, reassuring, or trying to fix the problem, Manjula said simply: "It sounds like you're going through a really tough time, Lucas. I can't imagine how hard it must be to feel this way."
- **Congruence.** As the conversation continued, Lucas mentioned feeling like he was going to be found out by his

colleagues, and they would see he was incompetent. This resonated with Manjula, who had felt the same way in the past, when she had started her career. Instead of hiding this, Manjula shared her own experience: "You know, Lucas, I've felt that way before too. It's really tough."

- **Unconditional positive regard.** Despite the heavy nature of the conversation, Manjula didn't judge or criticise Lucas. Instead, she reassured Lucas, saying: "I want you to know that it's okay to feel this way, and I'm here for you no matter what."

In this everyday conversation, Manjula was able to create a safe and supportive space for Lucas to express his feelings. Thinking about those three guiding principles before entering a conversation can be helpful in building a positive rapport. But it takes practice. It might be helpful to think about similar conversations you might have had in the past, and how you have (or have not) used the core conditions in your conversations. The more familiar you are with how to use them, the easier they will feel to deploy when needed.

REACT

An alternative to the core conditions is the REACT technique: a formal framework to help people have supportive and compassionate conversations about their mental health.

REACT stands for:

- **Recognise.** Use the risk factors in Chapter 6 to notice changes in behaviours that may indicate a change in wellbeing state.
- **Engage.** Start a conversation about wellbeing or mental health.

- **Actively listen**: Listen to what is being shared, making the sharer feel heard and understood.
- **Check risk.** Use the ASQ tool in Chapter 6 if needed.
- **Talk about specific actions.** Plan and encourage further support and next steps that can continue once the initial conversation has finished.

The technique was developed by experts in the UK and used to train managers and supervisors in the NHS. Research demonstrates that REACT training has increased managers' confidence when talking about and supporting mental health with their people.[7]

Remember Nikos in Chapter 6, who had just ended a committed long-term relationship and was not feeling himself. His boss, Darius, met him for a wellbeing check-in, and used the REACT technique to structure their conversation.

- **Recognise**. Darius had recognised that Nikos was behaving differently to usual. He noticed that he had stopped having lunch with the team, and seemed more withdrawn and disengaged. Darius understood that these changes in Nikos's behaviour were potential signs of poor mental health.
- **Engage**. Darius opts to approach Nikos in private and express his observations in a non-judgemental way, saying: "Nikos, I've noticed you've been a bit quiet lately, and we've not seen you at lunch often. Is everything all right?"
- **Actively listen**. Nikos opens up about his recent break-up, and how this has left him feeling depressed and alone. Darius doesn't interrupt or offer advice; instead, he actively listens and validates Nikos's experience with empathy.

He says: "It sounds like you're having a difficult time and dealing with a lot. This must be really hard."

- **Check risk**. Darius asks Nikos some gentle questions to assess whether he might be at risk of harm, such as: "Have you had any thoughts of hurting yourself?" If Nikos expresses any such thoughts, Darius can ask the suicide-screening questions (see Chapter 6) and, depending on the answers, escalate the situation to refer Nikos to appropriate mental health professionals immediately.

- **Talk about specific actions**. Finally, Darius discusses potential next steps with Nikos. He may suggest Nikos speaks with his general practitioner or makes use of any workplace counselling that's available. Darius thanks Nikos for sharing, and reassures him that seeking help is a sign of strength and that he will support him through this process.

ALGEE

The ALGEE method is a technique used in mental health first aid training.[8] The step-by-step process helps the listener to support someone in distress and ensure they receive practical help.

ALGEE stands for:

- **Assess** for risk of suicide or self-harm. You may feel nervous asking about risk, but if approached with sensitivity and composure, conversations about risk can be useful and validating. The suicide-screening questions outlined in Chapter 6 can guide conversations about risk, and support appropriate follow-up action.

- **Listen** non-judgementally. When having wellbeing conversations, give space for sharing and respond in a non-judgemental way. This involves responding without shaming or doubting what the person is sharing. For example, avoid phrases such as "It can't be that bad" or "Maybe you just misunderstood what was said." The listener needs to understand that what is being shared is the other person's valid reality and perspective at this time, and needs to be respected and accepted as such. Doing otherwise carries the risk that the person sharing will not feel heard.

- **Give** reassurance and information. It is vital to validate what someone is sharing. Often people may feel ashamed or dismissive of how they are feeling. For example, they may use phrases like "I'm just being dramatic" or "I shouldn't feel like this." Your reassurance will encourage more sharing. Providing information also supports sharing – for example, information about available support within your organisation or the common mental health difficulties that working adults can face.

- **Encourage** appropriate professional help. You may have initiated a wellbeing conversation, but it should not be the last. Wellbeing conversations are the first step for others to seek support, and should be used to encourage people to seek further support as needed.

- **Encourage** self-help and other support strategies. Wellbeing conversations can also suggest self-help strategies, like those we looked at in Chapter 5. Recommending supportive strategies in early conversations is useful because action against poor wellbeing can be taken almost immediately.

SOLER

The SOLER technique originated by Gerard Egan was developed for active listening in counselling situations.[9] However, SOLER can be applied to many conversations, and it is particularly useful when people are sharing sensitive or distressing information. Unlike the techniques above, it is more focused on the environment in which conversations take place.

For example, let's go back to Maribelle, a recently qualified teacher who is feeling burnout at work (see Chapter 6). Maribelle's colleague and fellow teacher Janice uses the SOLER technique to ask how she is doing.

SOLER stands for:

- **Sit squarely.** The focus here is on considering how the environment around you can help build a safe space. This includes thinking about how you (the listener) and the other person (the sharer) will sit to have the wellbeing conversation. Recommended practice is to sit face to face so that you can show that you are paying attention and listening. Have these conversations away from your desk, and avoid physical barriers between you.

  Janice and Maribelle have chosen to meet at the end of the school day in the staff room, as they know they are unlikely to be disturbed and can use the sofas to sit comfortably. Janice sits facing Maribelle to signal she is fully present.

- **Open posture.** Having an open posture leads on from sitting squarely. This involves keeping arms to the side rather than crossing arms over the body. Open posture communicates that you are ready and willing to listen.

  Janice sits with Maribelle and keeps her arms by her side and in her lap, with her legs uncrossed. These non-verbal cues communicate that Janice is open to hearing about Maribelle's experience and is not being defensive.

- **Lean forward.** When talking with others, it's important to convey interest and attention. When actively listening, it is natural to lean forward in conversations. By doing so, the sharer feels listened to and that their words are important.

    As Maribelle begins to talk, Janice finds herself leaning forward, keen to hear about her experience. Janice also finds herself nodding at what Maribelle is saying. This demonstrates to Maribelle that Janice is genuinely interested in her experience and wants to be actively engaged in her conversation.

- **Eye contact.** Maintaining eye contact when talking to others conveys interest and attention. Consistent eye contact (with occasional glances away) can foster trust and feelings of safety. Good eye contact can also help to validate the sharer's experience because it is a clear indication that the listener is paying attention.

    Throughout the conversation, Janice maintains good eye contact with Maribelle. Janice notices that Maribelle looks away often and so Janice holds a steady gaze to communicate focused listening.

- **Relax.** Being relaxed does not mean lounging or slouching but instead remaining relaxed in body and manner. This also applies to how the listener responds to what is being shared, minimising the chance of overreacting to someone's news and inadvertently judging what is being shared.

    Janice ensures that her body language is relaxed. She doesn't check the clock or appear rushed, signalling to Maribelle that she is here for her and is allowing Maribelle to express her feelings at her own pace.

TABLE 7 **The dos and don'ts of wellbeing conversations**

Do	Don't
Do: Find a quiet, private space, where people can't walk in accidentally.	**Don't**: Be on show, e.g. in a visible meeting room or the lunch room.
Do: Ensure there are no distractions. Switch off phone and email notifications.	**Don't**: Talk over the person sharing or interrupt, even if it is to share your own similar experience.
Do: Maintain good eye contact and open body language (nod, leave space to talk, make encouraging sounds).	**Don't**: Dismiss what is being shared.
	Don't: Invalidate or try to contradict what is being shared.
Do: Respect the pace of sharing.	**Don't**: Offer advice like "I did this ..." or "Why don't you do this?"
Do: Understand the limits of confidentiality.	
Do: Validate, paraphrase and act as a supportive listening ear.	**Don't**: Use "should" or "must" when discussing next steps.
Do: Be empathic.	**Don't**: Expect people to tell you everything. Avoid over-questioning or being nosy.
Do: Be aware of the limitations of the support you can offer.	**Don't**: Promise anything, including actions or keeping information confidential.
Do: Encourage further support (professional or employment-based).	
	Don't: Be judgemental.
Do: Ask for clarification if you are unsure about anything that has been shared.	**Don't**: Overreact.
	Don't: Shut down conversations about wellbeing.

Although these models and frameworks can help, there is no perfect way to have a wellbeing conversation. These conversations are not tick-box exercises where you tick off each topic. Nor are they therapy sessions, where people are expected to bare all. But there are some clear dos and don'ts that you can bear in mind, summarised in Table 7. Remember that wellbeing conversations are open and honest discussions about someone's current situation and the steps that can be taken for support.

Tools for supporting others

Empathy maps

An empathy map is a tool used to understand the needs of a group of people. Some readers may be familiar with empathy maps in an organisational sense (for example, identifying customer needs). They can also be used to support and understand team members, and are particularly useful for understanding collective perspective and experiences. You can use these maps to gain insight into what a team is thinking, saying, feeling and doing, for example, about a specific project or departmental change. Empathy maps can provide valuable insights into a team's motivations, frustrations and needs, which might then inform strategies for improving team dynamics and performance, all of which will support wellbeing.

Empathy maps can be generated in four stages.

1. **Defining scope and goals.** What is the purpose of doing an empathy map? And what or who will it cover? For example, a team could form an empathy map to understand and respond to departmental changes.

2. **Data collection.** The next stage involves collecting information from the team and others relevant to the goal. This data may come from surveys, meeting discussions, interviews or focus group questioning, or observations and line management discussions.

3. **Populate the map.** Using the data collected, start to populate the different sections of the map, including what people are thinking, feeling, saying and doing to provide a holistic overview of the team's current experience.

4. **Reflection.** Reflect on the map to uncover insights that will initiate possible changes to practice.

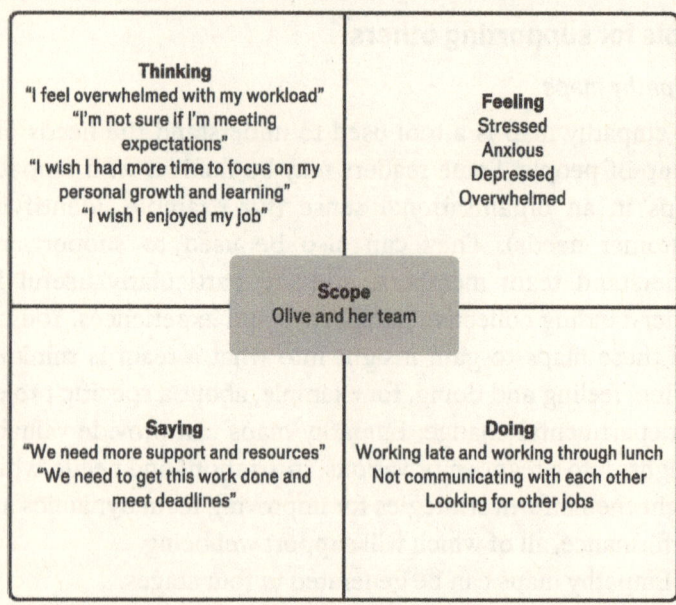

Thinking
"I feel overwhelmed with my workload"
"I'm not sure if I'm meeting expectations"
"I wish I had more time to focus on my personal growth and learning"
"I wish I enjoyed my job"

Feeling
Stressed
Anxious
Depressed
Overwhelmed

Scope
Olive and her team

Saying
"We need more support and resources"
"We need to get this work done and meet deadlines"

Doing
Working late and working through lunch
Not communicating with each other
Looking for other jobs

Figure 13: **Empathy map: Olive and her team**

To understand this in practice, let's return to Olive (Chapter 6), a project manager with a reduced team following redundancy. Olive decides to check in with her team using an empathy map, inviting all members to participate. (See Figure 13.)

After reflecting on the empathy map, Olive has a deeper emotional understanding of her team, and uses this to make productive changes. She initiates check-ins at each team meeting to encourage non-work sharing and connection. She also plans to ask individual members about their wellbeing using the REACT technique, and find out more about any external support that may be useful.

Behavioural activation and job design

As discussed in Chapter 5, the basis of behavioural activation is the idea that increasing activity has the potential to improve mood, as it allows for greater chances to experience pleasure, connection or achievement. In daily life, behavioural activation can occur when seeing friends, engaging with hobbies and reaching personal goals. It can also be adapted and used to help and support others at work.

Behavioural activation can be used to balance tasks that are more draining with more engagement in activities that bring a sense of accomplishment and pleasure, which can help improve mood and reduce symptoms of depression. It will make work more attractive, improve the mood of individuals, which then trickles up to benefit the entire team.

It's particularly helpful when reviewing job design, helping you to understand the energy costs and gains for specific tasks and activities. You can consider what are most draining and, in contrast, what are the more energising activities, both of which can promote wellbeing at work. Understanding and examining the occupational load (and costs or gains) across a typical working week is useful in uncovering the relationship between work activities and wellbeing state.

Using a three-step approach, let's look at Jordan as he reviews his job design. Jordan is an events coordinator for a university. He spends his work week planning activities for students and staff and managing external partners who use the university buildings to hold events. Jordan has noticed that his motivation for work has dipped and some days he dreads going into the office. As a result, he wants to review his job.

Step 1. Review

The first step Jordan takes is to review his job description. This involves checking to see if the description is accurate and relevant to his role, and making sure all tasks and expected responsibilities are included and required for his day-to-day role. Jordan also checks to see if all responsibilities can be completed in a typical working week. Jordan has been in his role for five years, and his team has expanded since he started, so he checks to see if his managerial responsibilities are reflected in his job description. He also notices that he now spends a considerable amount of time building partnerships with external companies rather than focusing solely on the university staff and population. Jordan adds these tasks to his job description and removes any irrelevant or out-of-date tasks that he has now delegated to others.

Step 2. Evaluate

Once Jordan is content that his job description is accurate, he evaluates each task and responsibility in terms of:

- energy required to complete each task, and whether this is realistic
- estimated time cost over a working week
- level of positive or negative experience and feelings associated with tasks
- level of social connection required, and if this feels agreeable or draining
- level of pride or achievement upon completion.

Jordan recognises that he feels apprehensive about tasks centred around external partners and, because he feels isolated from the rest of his team, he feels he has to carry the responsibility alone. He notices that he enjoyed running the student events and frequently felt a sense of achievement when they went successfully. Jordan feels reassured that he can confidently complete most tasks within his working week.

Step 3. Adapt

Jordan reviews the current scheduling of his tasks and activity across the working week and makes changes to encourage:

- a spread of high and lower energy tasks, to avoid over-exhaustion and promote a balanced working week
- opportunities for social connection at least once a day, with time aside for lone or focused work
- room to share achievements with others
- time to support learning, development and growth.

For Jordan this meant he invited some of his team to meetings with external partners to reduce lone working. He also ensured that he could attend at least one student event every two weeks to feel a sense of pride. After implementing these changes, Jordan noticed he felt less drained after work and looked forward to collaborating with others. He took his review one step further by encouraging his team to review their own job descriptions and reflect on how they could make changes to their working to promote wellbeing.

SMART goals

SMART goals are a popular tool for effective goal setting, and can be applied to many areas of life. They can support wellbeing either explicitly by being focused on wellbeing (for example, *I want to feel connected at work*) or implicitly by focusing on goals that provide an opportunity for achievement and growth (for example, *I want to develop my coding skills*). SMART goals are achievable and not overwhelming, both of which improve wellbeing. SMART goals can also be set for a team, to encourage collaboration and shared achievement.

SMART stands for:

- **Specific**. What is the goal? Include as much detail as possible and be specific about what you are trying to achieve and do.
- **Measurable**. How will progress towards the goal be measured? This may be via changes in behaviours or actions. Will the result be perceivable to others?
- **Achievable**. Is the goal achievable? Although challenging, will you be able to accomplish the end result? Will the goal be achievable in the context of usual duties and tasks, or will other activities have to be replaced?
- **Relevant**. Is the goal realistic without causing unnecessary overwhelm? Is the goal appropriate and relevant to your role and wider organisational goals?
- **Time-bound**. When does the goal need to be achieved? Providing a deadline helps to focus the goal. It may be useful to set the deadline for your next appraisal or check-in to encourage you to make regular progress.

SMART goals can be especially useful for people who work on their own, such as entrepreneurs or independent practitioners within larger networks. For example, Natasha works as an independent accountant having recently completed her training. After gaining a handful of clients, she worries that her career potential has plateaued. Her client base is stable, but hasn't expanded in the last six months and this is making her anxious about her long-term financial security. Natasha wants to increase her client base so she can significantly increase her earnings.

Using the SMART goal format, she can break down her goal into objective and feasible steps.

- **Specific**. I want to increase my client base by gaining five additional clients.
- **Measurable**. The goal will be achieved when I have five new clients.
- **Achievable**. By investing time in marketing and social media, and using existing professional networks, I believe I can increase my client base.
- **Relevant**. By limiting my goal to just five new clients, I am keeping my goal manageable. It also aligns with my longer-term ambition of growing my business.
- **Time-bound**. I have set myself a time limit of four months, as this is when my room rental contract is up for review, so that I know whether to extend my contract or think about shared work space instead.

Keeping safe when supporting others

People vary in the extent to which they feel comfortable addressing topics related to wellbeing. Some may find these conversations natural, and initiate interactions with ease; others may find it helpful to stick to the step-by-step models as a guide for wellbeing conversations. There is no right or wrong approach.

It is, however, likely that these conversations will include distressing topics, thoughts and emotions. Therefore, as a listener, you need clear boundaries for wellbeing interactions. For example, have practical boundaries on where and when wellbeing conversations will take place (i.e. at work, during work hours), and make sure the role, scope and limitations of a listener are understood and communicated. Even a simple reminder about not being a professional can help the person sharing to understand and have realistic expectations. Having and communicating boundaries when supporting others will protect both the person sharing and the person listening, as there will be clear and agreed expectations about the availability and limitations of support. Healthy boundaries also prevent the listener from becoming overly attached to the other person and what is shared.

When you are placed in the role of a helper or listener, it is typical to experience feelings of high responsibility and pressure to fix someone or make them feel better. This is particularly common if the person in distress is asking you to solve their problems, demonstrating helplessness, or demanding more and more time from you. However, supporting someone in this way is unsustainable and will compromise your own wellbeing. It is inappropriate and ultimately detrimental to everyone involved.

Conversely, some people may not welcome wellbeing conversations. You may encounter defensiveness, overwhelm or anxiety. This may be particularly true for those who have never spoken about their wellbeing before or have a tendency towards self-criticism; they may see an act of support as a criticism of their ability to cope. In these circumstances, following the guidance for wellbeing conversations will be useful and seeking professional guidance is recommended. It is also possible that these and other situations will be emotionally taxing. Understandably, listening to anxious thoughts, detrimental behaviours or depressive feelings can have a huge impact on the wellbeing of a listener. When this happens, it's important to be mindful and check in with yourself regularly, engaging with self-care and support as necessary.

Being aware of your own limitations, mood and boundaries will protect against listener fatigue and safeguard personal wellbeing. Don't forget the first circle of WBQ, which is to prioritise self-awareness and self-care. This will ensure that you are in a better position to support yourself and others.

Supporting the mental health of others in the workplace is crucial and can be guided with the simple frameworks we share in this chapter. Encouraging open discussions about mental health can help people feel more comfortable and supported. A psychologically safe team can provide a safe space for colleagues to share their experiences and seek help. Behavioural activation and SMART goals can be effective techniques to help colleagues manage their wellbeing.

Mental health is, of course, a spectrum, and everyone's experience is unique. You might not be able to understand the way other people feel even when you have experienced something that seems similar. People at work need to be supported at every stage of the mental health spectrum, whether they are simply a little more stressed than usual this week or have a diagnosed mental health condition.

8
Managing and leading with wellbeing intelligence

Rashida has been the HR director for a medium-sized catering company for the past two years. In contrast with her previous boss, her current CEO openly cares for the employees' mental health. The CEO consciously engages in wellbeing checks, taking mental health days, and sharing her experiences with others. Rashida sees these actions across all areas of the organisation, as those in leadership and management positions exhibit wellbeing-focused behaviour. Teams feel psychologically safe and, as a consequence, learn better and faster. Conflicts are solved quickly through collaboration and are seen as opportunities for learning and improvement. The focus on wellbeing has given people like Rashida the chance to enjoy their work instead of seeing it as the means to an end.

In addition to benefiting from this environment as an employee, Rashida has developed her leadership skills in this environment to support her team: she has become more careful about organising her workload to preserve her wellbeing and uses this knowledge to help other team members. She has built better connections with her colleagues, participates in their growth, and helps to get the best out of them. Wellbeing intelligence has led not only to mutual care but also to better performance, for herself, others and the organisation.

As Rashida's story shows, although wellbeing intelligence is the responsibility of everyone at work, leaders and managers have a special responsibility to set the tone and role model behaviours and actions that support wellbeing positive organisations. This chapter examines some core management principles with wellbeing intelligence front of mind, exploring how a more holistic approach to wellbeing is crucial to people's workplace interactions more generally. In previous chapters, we have focused on how to manage issues directly related to wellbeing. This chapter takes a step back to look at how wellbeing intelligence can inform management and leadership in a broader sense.

That matters. By incorporating wellbeing-intelligent practices as a cultural norm, individuals, teams and organisations can benefit beyond their positive impact on mental health: wellbeing-intelligent managers who are content and happy with their lives and environment have been found to be more effective at work.[1] Unsurprisingly, a trickle-down effect can boost team morale and cohesion. Think of your own workplace: it will undoubtedly be the case that when your boss is happy, things tend to run more smoothly.

It's not a given, though, that wellbeing-intelligent individuals are necessarily good managers. It's important to understand the connections between wellbeing intelligence and management skills more broadly, and how the two interact. The three circles of wellbeing intelligence (see Chapter 3) show how wellbeing-intelligent managers can build skills at all three levels. At the individual level, wellbeing-intelligent individuals can motivate themselves and others. They can also positively influence team dynamics, leadership and an organisation's culture. Because of that, wellbeing intelligence is a future-proofing skill that is especially important for managers and leaders.

Wellbeing intelligence and motivation

One of the core skills of a good manager is the ability to motivate others. Much has been written on motivation at work, but rarely with wellbeing in mind. Wellbeing intelligence is crucial in this as there is much overlap between the skills of wellbeing intelligence and the capacity to motivate others.

Praising colleagues' achievements

Recognising someone's accomplishments, efforts and hard work can boost their self-esteem and confidence. Self-esteem and confidence in turn drive wellbeing. High self-esteem and self-efficacy are crucial when the task at hand is challenging, and when the demanding nature of the work has the potential to be discouraging, and thus a source of stress and depression. Validating other people's efforts not only builds wellbeing; it also reinforces the behaviours that led to the success. Even a small word of praise can increase motivation to perform well in future. The telecom company Three, for example, has a webpage on its intranet that enables people to send a colleague a digital "thank you" note. This may sound gimmicky, but it fosters a virtuous cycle in which people recognise the contributions of others and see their own efforts acknowledged.

Setting incremental goals

Setting and achieving small, incremental goals can provide a sense of progress and control, which are both key drivers of motivation. But it can also reduce feelings of overwhelm or stress as large tasks or projects feel more manageable. Goal setting allows people to see themselves growing in achievement and competence over time, which can be very satisfying and encouraging. If you ask a team to build a rocket to go the moon, even the most highly skilled engineers with the best resources will find the task daunting, and easily get discouraged if they do not see themselves reaching incremental goals along the way. However, if they break down the task and start with small achievable goals, they will soon build the confidence and courage needed for the bigger goal.

Giving autonomy

Autonomy empowers people to make their own choices and take responsibility for outcomes and their own learning. Feeling entrusted and in control boosts employees' self-esteem. However, autonomy must be balanced with appropriate capacity and confidence: too much autonomy can overwhelm people if they do not have the right support, guidance or skills. Think about a school tutor being given autonomy to solve conflicts between students: they will get a chance to grow their skills and better understand the students, as well as gaining satisfaction from solving problems by themselves. Yet if they are not given the time or the space to reflect on the experience of dealing with and responding to students in conflict, to get support when they first take on the responsibility, and to learn by doing, then that autonomy will instead become a source of stress.

Providing career growth and development opportunities

Opportunities for advancement and learning new skills can make a job more engaging and satisfying. Opportunities for growth give a sense of future direction which can increase motivation. It addresses feelings of stagnation or dissatisfaction, both potential sources of stress or burnout. Equally, learning new skills can provide mental stimulation, achieving the same objective of helping individuals to see themselves growing. Imagine someone who has been in the same job for a decade with little chance for development; they are frustrated, feel stuck and often feel quite depressed. They need help to see how they can develop and progress.

Why those four practices work

These four practices are based on some of the most empirically rooted thinking about motivation: self-determination theory. This theory recognises three essential drivers of motivation. People need to:

1. be given autonomy to perform their work
2. be able to express and grow their competence
3. feel connected with others and cared for.

And while those approaches can boost both wellbeing and motivation, their absence might have negative implications. They also suggest that being well often means being motivated and vice versa. It's possible, of course, for demotivated people to be well and have strong mental health. But feeling constrained at work, stuck in terms of growth, or feeling invisible is the sort of work experience that might ultimately have a negative impact on wellbeing.

Needs-based theories of motivation, such as Maslow's hierarchy of needs (see Chapter 1) offer another important lesson: people might be demotivated because their fundamental need for wellbeing is not being met, or their wellbeing is low because their need for motivation is ignored. Motivation and wellbeing can be conditional on each other; therefore it is crucial that managers actively address the motivation of others if they also want them to be well.

Improving wellbeing is also often a question of motivation. As outlined in chapters 4 and 5, people who experience anxiety may need to challenge their thoughts and break maintenance cycles by facing what they fear. They may have to engage in behavioural activation by purposefully doing things they enjoy to improve their mood. This all takes motivation. To some extent, the motivation to address mental health challenges is similar to the motivation to perform at work; it depends on being able to see light at the end of the tunnel. If people can see themselves reaching their objectives and their efforts paying off, they will remain committed to those efforts in future.

Wellbeing intelligence and team dynamics

Wellbeing is crucial to the functioning of teams, not only because team members can support each other but also because teams that experience higher levels of wellbeing perform better. One of the foundational studies in this field concerns television production teams at the BBC. Researchers found a positive association between the mental health of teams and their potential for creativity.[2] Connectedness and belongingness are also driven by wellbeing. A happy team, where people feel energised by each other, is likely to perform better.

Team identity

Many aspects of team dynamics are fuelled by and fuel wellbeing. One of these is team identity – the sense of what makes a team unique and creates a shared sense of belonging. A strong team identity makes members feel that their own identity overlaps with the wider group: their work and collaboration within the team will be positively reflected in themselves. The feeling of being part of something larger than yourself drives a willingness to work towards common goals. So the link between wellbeing and team identity is straightforward. If team members have good mental health, they are more likely to socialise, create interpersonal bonds that go beyond work relationships, and engage deeply with each other and their work. Good mental health also boosts interpersonal trust: if people can rely on each other, they also believe they can achieve a lot more.

So how can managers develop and encourage team identity? Here are just some things to try.

- Develop, foster and communicate a shared vision, goal and values.
- Celebrate team achievements and milestones, in person or via email.
- Make clear and deliberate efforts to value input and contribution from all team members, understanding individual roles in the team and their common goals.
- Foster connections by creating spaces and moments to socialise and create bonds, for example with a weekly lunch. This will help develop trust and open communication between team members. Members will feel psychologically safe; they will feel able to talk about what can be improved and changed without the fear of being judged.
- Shape the identity of the team themselves by branding it, perhaps including it in an email signature.

Let's take the example of a marketing team responsible for snack foods. The team is newly formed following a company expansion, and the team members haven't worked together before. At the first team meeting, their manager takes the time to outline the vision she has for the team, and shares details of the team's upcoming project, introducing a common sense of purpose. Members are invited to brainstorm the values they feel important as they form their team, focusing on creativity and respectful collaboration as they begin to work together. In subsequent meetings, their manager takes the time to give an update on how their project is moving forwards and to celebrate the team's success each time they reach a new milestone. This has encouraged deeper connections within the team, leading to better motivation and engagement.

Research shows that this kind of strong team identification can translate diversity and learning into performance.[3] A multidisciplinary team – for example, a project team with people from different parts of an organisation – might have regular disagreements. But if the members of the team see themselves as part of a greater purpose, they become more aware of each other and ready to step away when they realise someone else might hold the right skills to address an issue. People will be more willing to share ideas and support their colleagues. The alignment – how each member understands their role in relation to the roles of others and the overall objective and purpose of the team – will also be greatly improved.

Team identity also reinforces wellbeing to create a virtuous cycle. Even in tough times, the team will be propelled by its sense of purpose, and team members' wellbeing will be preserved. The team will have better emotional and mental resources to face such situations.

Conflict resolution

Wellbeing intelligence within teams is also crucial for resolving conflict. Even in well managed and wellbeing-intelligent teams like Rashida's, there is still the potential for unhealthy disagreement. However, a happy team is more likely to deal with conflict respectfully and share any learning from conflict with others. In Rashida's team, for example, people have been arguing about what benefits should be provided to the staff: some team members think mental health support should be covered by the employee health insurance plan; others believe their in-house psychologist should provide it. If Rashida's team did not share a strong team identity, this type of disagreement would have the potential to turn into interpersonal conflict. But because the team members manage and support their own and each others' wellbeing, and have built good connections between them, their communication is improved and respectful. So the quarrel about employee benefits is about how to do the work best, rather than who is involved or any personal feelings. If conflicts arise, they are more likely to be passed over quickly as misunderstandings, and the team can move on faster.

Wellbeing intelligence plays a pivotal role in bolstering the morale of teams, fostering team cohesion and enhancing overall team effectiveness. A team fuelled by wellbeing intelligence will also create a sense of belonging and mutual respect among team members. When team members feel valued and cared for, they are more likely to be engaged, motivated and productive, thereby enhancing team effectiveness. This in turn helps team members to complete the virtuous circle and cultivate their own wellbeing intelligence.

Wellbeing intelligence and leadership

Most of this book has focused on management, and on how individuals can direct others on an individual and team basis. This section looks at broader approaches to creating a strategic vision to inspire and drive other to give their best at work – skills often associated with leadership.

Leadership and the importance of different leadership styles is one of the largest fields of business research, explored in all types of books and dedicated academic journals. Understanding effective leadership styles matters to wellbeing for one simple reason: when leaders are stressed, followers are too.[4] The wellbeing of leaders affects the wellbeing of followers, in one way or another. For example, destructive leadership, such as aggressive and hostile behaviour or excessive control, has been found to generate more stress and anxiety.

In contrast, transformational leadership is one of the most researched and proven positive leadership styles. Transformational leadership is often explained using the four Is.

1. **Intellectual stimulation.** Transformational leaders support people to grow by enabling them to think about complex problems and giving them the satisfaction of solving the problems.

2. **Inspirational motivation.** Transformational leaders motivate their followers by inspiring them to look at a longer-term horizon, and at what they can achieve collectively.

3. **Idealised influence.** Transformational leaders are role models. Their behaviours can be followed and trusted.

4. **Individualised consideration**. Individualised consideration requires leaders to make their followers feel cared for and for the followers to care for their leaders. It is about paying attention to all individuals and making them feel heard and seen. Such leadership ability plays a central role in organisational performance and job satisfaction.

The link between those four Is and wellbeing is obvious. Being able to see progress and see ourselves growing contributes to wellbeing. Motivation keeps people focused on what they need to do. And positive role models help people deal with the reality of the workplace. For example, leaders who can show vulnerability towards mental health issues and strong boundaries between their work and their personal life will help their followers build a better work hygiene, and increase their wellbeing. Happy leaders make more effective ones, because happy leaders are more likely to be transformational leaders – and research has found that transformational leaders boost their employees' mental health.[5] Good leadership leads to good mental health, leading to good organisational performance.

Emotional intelligence is also a core positive leadership trait. The capacity of leaders to perceive their own emotions and the emotions of others, and adapt their behaviours accordingly, makes them more effective.

Both individualised consideration and emotional competence interact with wellbeing intelligence. Understanding people's wellbeing challenges is an important part of individualised consideration. To relate to others, leaders need to understand what affects their approach and ability to work. Only on this basis can leaders genuinely appreciate their colleagues and put themselves in others' shoes to build empathy. Being aware of your own emotions, and wellbeing is crucial for this. Positive leader–follower interactions promote mental health, not only for the leaders but also for their followers.[6]

The opposite is also true. Stressed and anxious leaders are more likely to fall into toxic behaviours, which in turn have an impact on the behaviour of their followers. Consider the example of a volatile leader in a financial services setting, leading people with responsibilities on a trading floor. Market shifts affect his mood, often manifested by him shouting at colleagues indiscriminately. As we have seen, followers look to their leaders for cues about how to behave. If the behaviour modelled is a toxic one, this often causes a contagion of bad practice. Other employees will start behaving this way, thinking it is all right to do so. Moral and mental health will plummet and the organisation will suffer from what has become a new norm.

Beyond behaviours, simple negative prejudice about what makes a good leader in a specific organisation or industry can become a self-fulfilling prophecy. Expectations that a leader needs to be "assertive", "opinionated" or "persistent" can get in the way of wellbeing intelligence. A wellbeing-intelligent breed of leaders might not fit with traditional expectations of how a leader is expected to behave in more traditional, high-pressure sectors. Paradoxically, these environments are where wellbeing-intelligent leaders are most needed.

There is also negative prejudice around what "makes" a leader. An experiment conducted by Fast Company asked children below the age of ten to draw a "leader".[7] Most of the children were not fazed and started drawing their teacher or their parents. Importantly, they were likely to draw themselves, in contrast with most adults, who would not have the confidence to do so.

Leadership is a broad word with multiple meanings and many interpretations; individuals, depending on their background, perceive leadership from very different angles. Many want to imagine themselves as leaders but might be prevented by negative feedback and experience. They also compare themselves with whoever they have been led by, and consider whether they can fill similar shoes. This again emphasises the importance of providing people with role models that can inspire their leadership style – and breaking the mould of what we imagine to be a leader to encourage the development of leaders focused on mental health.

So where to start to break the mould? At the top. A virtuous leadership style at the top is likely to affect behaviours at all levels because of the power of leaders as role models. A CEO's experience with mental health sets the tone and the culture for the whole organisation. They can give visibility to mental health issues by sharing their own experience. Matthew Cooper, the CEO of Silicon Valley start-up EarnUp, stepped away from his firm in August 2020 because of anxiety and depression. He talked openly about the mental health challenges he faced. Such openness has a huge cultural impact and contributes to the normalisation of mental health issues, making them more likely to be detected and addressed. Leaders must be mental health advocates by sharing their experiences and encouraging others to do so. And to do so, they need to understand those experiences and go back to the first circle of wellbeing: leaders need to be aware of their own mental health so they can support their followers and their organisations.

Leaders who care about others and use self-care as a learning opportunity to understand and support their colleagues better can create goodwill around them. When people feel supported, or feel they would be supported if needed, they are more likely to reciprocate by supporting those paying attention to their emotional and mental state. They are more likely to go that extra mile and act as engaged and committed organisational citizens.

Wellbeing intelligence in practice: acknowledge, respond, change

The ARC model – acknowledge, respond and change – encapsulates three vital skills that people need in order to exercise their wellbeing intelligence at work (see Figure 14). It encapsulates how the principles of wellbeing intelligence can inform day-to-day approaches to management. It's a useful shorthand for managers and leaders and a way for them to

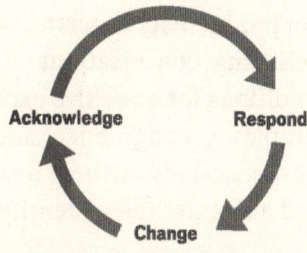

Figure 14: **ARC: acknowledge, respond and change**

prioritise wellbeing intelligence and role model wellbeing-intelligent behaviours.

Here's how it can be used.

Acknowledge poor mental health

The first stage is about recognising another's distress, fostering awareness and validating their feelings. Tools like the hot cross bun map (see Chapter 4) can help people to identify emotional and mental states. Through open conversations, people can help others to recognise and break unhealthy maintenance cycles, contributing to improved mental health. They can also help them work out how they might be stuck in a way of thinking, damaging their wellbeing. Presenting them with the different cognitive reframing approach can be eye-opening.

Respond to signs of emotional distress

Once a problem has been acknowledged, responding involves facilitating discussions about emotional wellbeing and empathising with an individual's experiences. Active, non-judgemental listening can create a supportive environment. Normalising mental health conversations reduces stigma, encouraging a positive workplace culture that prioritises employee support over productivity concerns. We shared a range of approaches to wellbeing conversations in Chapter 7, and looked at the core conditions for a positive exchange as defined by psychologists: empathy, congruence and unconditional positive regard. Those discussions can help foster psychological safety in the team, and a positive team identity.

Change behaviour

The next stage is to help people to change their thinking and behaviours, using tools like cognitive reframing, encouraging others to challenge unhelpful thoughts, and promoting more realistic perspectives. Behavioural activation, encouraging pleasurable and meaningful activities, can have a positive impact on employees' mental health. This can be set up as a principle at work. People need to recognise patterns, communicate needs and actively participate in the process, but managers and leaders also need to provide the right culture for support and encouragement.

By applying the ARC model, managers can play a crucial role in fostering a workplace culture that prioritises mental health, contributing to overall wellbeing and productivity in the workplace. Importantly, the ARC model stresses the learning aspect: wellbeing intelligence is a muscle that can be grown only if practised. Triggering positive change in yourself or others can help you to acknowledge and respond to wellbeing issues better.

Wellbeing intelligence as future proofing

Future proofing is crucial for anyone who is responsible for setting the course for an organisation or a collective endeavour. However, setting a vision can be hard when the world is changing at such a fast pace. From the shift to home or remote working to the rise of artificial intelligence (AI), changes to working practices, how we interact with colleagues, and the nature of the work itself make it hard to set a course in what might seem like uncharted waters.

Wellbeing intelligence is a way to be better prepared for an uncertain future because it makes people more resilient to change. Leaders who cultivate their own wellbeing will be in a better position to learn from their mistakes, and adapt their ways of doing things even when emotionally costly. Any stress caused by the need for change, individually or organisationally, will not have to add to an existing state of stress. They will be able to take decisions with a cooler head. Such leaders are also in a better position to inspire their team to stay committed and adaptable in challenging times, as they have addressed mental health issues upstream. Even when mental health is affected by change, whether it is a change in the organisation (e.g. a merger) or in the environment (e.g. an economic crisis), wellbeing-intelligent leaders have built the resources to understand the effect of change on their mental health and on the mental health of their team. With the tools we shared in this book they can address this effect.

When people can analyse how they experience change and the impact it might have on their mental health, they can more readily accept and adjust their approach as change happens. They can move to another job more easily, or learn new skills from other people or machines. Learning new skills may even be seen as an opportunity for growth that reinforces wellbeing. A review of the literature suggests that in most cases when individuals learn to be more proficient in their role (e.g. learning to use new software), they develop better relationships with their colleagues, and ultimately improve their wellbeing.[8]

Technological advances, like AI, are not always a threat to

wellbeing. Imagine tools fuelled by machine learning that can predict the parts of the organisation that might be most exposed to wellbeing issues; a person's connection and relationships within an organisation can be used to predict the likelihood of them quitting their job.[9] Data about workload or reduced interactions in person might give an indication of a lack of wellbeing. Such technologies are not without their challenges – for example, in relation to confidentiality – but the potential is there.

Wellbeing intelligence doesn't just help improve awareness of your own and other people's wellbeing. It also helps foster better management and leadership. It can improve team dynamics, boost skills and foster adaptability to future changes. It feeds and is fed by emotional intelligence, helping people to communicate effectively, build connections and adapt to the needs of those they lead. It enhances resilience, helping people to navigate challenges and changes with grace and grit.

Wellbeing also leads to better decision-making and adaptability, fostering strategic thinking that benefits both individuals and organisations. It enhances social relationships, creating a supportive network that can assist during times of change. In essence, wellbeing intelligence informs many aspects of management and leadership. It is indissociable from the question of motivation and team building on a day-to-day basis, but can also provide the keys to looking at a longer-term horizon.

PART 4

The third circle of wellbeing intelligence: a wellbeing-intelligent organisation

Parts 2 and 3 explored the two first circles of wellbeing intelligence: understanding and helping yourself and others. However, even the most wellbeing-intelligent people and teams can feel isolated if their approach is at odds with the rest of their organisation. Wellbeing intelligence is fuelled by our care for ourselves and others, but the organisational context must also support wellbeing, rather than act as an obstacle. Sometimes wellbeing-intelligent workers can feel as if they are swimming against the tide.

Cynthia leads the delivery of support services in a charity called CARING, which assists people experiencing homelessness. She has a routine to monitor and protect her wellbeing, especially during the hectic periods for her organisation: the winter months. She notices when she finds herself being overwhelmed and can detect a growing sense of anxiety in herself from miles away, so will engage in grounding and mindfulness activities as often as she needs. Cynthia directly supports her team members and looks out for their mental health. She understands that, when work is meaningful and impactful, it is easy to feel consumed by it and end up doing more and more until it becomes impossible to do anything else. She helps the people she manages to create clear boundaries between their work and their personal lives; they can only help others if they are well themselves. Yet despite her high wellbeing intelligence, her organisation continues to ask its employees for more, with the board and the other top managers piling up pressure and not understanding why people are taking sick leave and leaving in droves. They see the work as so crucial for the beneficiaries that they have forgotten about caring for their employees.

Not all organisations are like this. More often than not, wellbeing-intelligent employees make a wellbeing-intelligent organisation, or at least push it in this direction. To scale up positive wellbeing change, and broaden the support for positive wellbeing practices, many will promote wellbeing more widely, particular in psychologically safe environments. That's where understanding and prioritising individual and team wellbeing can trigger broader systemic change and inspire new organisational approaches.

But some wellbeing issues require higher-level support than an individual manager alone can provide. An extreme example is what happened at France Télécom, the French national telecom company that was hit by a wave of suicides from 2006 to 2011. Although the legal process considered 19 suicides and 12 attempts, many more were reported by the unions. This terrible situation has often been attributed to the company's privatisation and restructuring. Many of the managers felt lost and unsure what to do and how to support their employees. This is when the third circle of wellbeing comes into play: wellbeing-intelligent organisations, creating better wellbeing and resilience at an organisational level.

At the opposite end of the spectrum, the healthcare company Johnson & Johnson was one of the first movers in the wellbeing space in the 1950s. Early on, the firm realised the importance of integrating wellbeing into its organisational culture. It introduced a range of new wellbeing policies and practices, including employee resource groups, apps, training and support programmes. Each programme is regularly evaluated and improved.

Awareness around wellbeing has been raised through targeted campaigns. Leaders have shown the way by discussing their mental health issues (what Johnson & Johnson call "mental health diplomats"). Wellbeing issues have become normalised and freely talked about between employees; it has become an integral part of the company's culture.

Part 4 takes a strategic and organisational perspective on wellbeing and shows how to lead change for a more supportive workplace. We first look at corporate culture: how you can promote and integrate norms and values that promote wellbeing. It's often said that a culture amplifies the work of people: we believe that when you have a good culture promoting interactions and expectations that align with wellbeing, the need for people to preserve and encourage wellbeing in isolation becomes less urgent because the culture begins to reinforce wellbeing messages.

The right policies and practical forms of support are also important, whether they're about wellbeing pre-emption, detection or remedy. Managers and leaders can and should lead the charge on those issues, but a culture shift can also come from the bottom up with employees who experience wellbeing issues putting those issues on the agenda for their managers and their organisations. The important thing is that organisations take seriously their responsibility for practices and programmes that will contribute to making wellbeing an integral part of how they operate.

9

A wellbeing culture

In the serene outskirts of a mid-size city sit the offices of QuantumTech, one of the emerging leaders in the field of quantum computing. The spacious glass-walled offices and gardens make employees cherish their days at work. But more than the space, they enjoy seeing colleagues whom they consider friends. Top executives walk around the cafeteria and offices like everybody else. People feel valued and heard, and are comfortable telling their colleagues that they are having a bad day, or that personal challenges are clouding their mind at work. Talking about emotions, feeling and wellbeing is normalised and people genuinely care for each other. Yet nobody could put their finger on what exactly was making them feel so comfortable.

Organisational culture can feel intangible, difficult to define and explain. But, as QuantumTech shows, it's an intangible and crucial part of wellbeing intelligence at an organisational level: the role played by corporate and workplace culture in promoting wellbeing. But before we get into that, let's address a simple question: what is organisational culture? If it's intangible, how can we actually "see" it?

There are many ways to encourage people to work together and collaborate. To do so, people need to understand the expected behaviours and values that drive their collective endeavours.

This is what is implicitly conveyed by organisational culture. For most of it, organisational culture is not always explicit and will emerge even without conscious acknowledgement. Yet it has the power to drive wellbeing at scale.

Organisational culture is often defined as the set of shared values, beliefs, norms and practices that make each organisation unique. Those values, beliefs and norms drive the perception of things like risk appetite, failure, hierarchy or conflict, among many others. Those values and norms guide behaviours, and tell members implicitly what is accepted and expected, encouraged and valued. Culture is not only intangible; it is often there to explain the unexplainable: the way an office is organised; the way people greet each other when they meet in the workplace; the meaning of the portrait of the founder hanging above the doors; the choice of yellow as the firm's colour.

An organisation's culture can work for and against wellbeing. Positive, supportive cultures enable wellbeing best practices to be reproduced and maintained. But the opposite is also true: culture may reinforce practices that directly harm wellbeing. For example, cultures where the expectation is that people stay late and work long hours are often at odds with people's self-care needs for adequate rest and sleep.

The values, beliefs, norms and practices that constitute the organisational culture tend to (or should) reinforce each other. For example, an organisation that fights climate change and values sustainable practices is unlikely to provide single-use plastics in the company canteen or explicitly support air travel for business meetings. An organisation where people are expected to answer their emails at any time of the day in record time has to rely on the right IT and phone support for its people to do so. Beyond the intangible, there can also be concrete manifestations of a culture, such as people's dress codes, the design of the office space or a building, and the characteristics of the founders.

The culture of homeless support at Cynthia's charity CARING is one where the expectation is that workers should go above and beyond because their service users need them so much. These kinds of expectations and principles are the basis on which work norms are built. At CARING, it is frowned upon to leave early to pick up a child who is sick at school ("Those left on the street cannot wait!"), or not to be available during the weekend when an emergency arises. The office of CARING has very little human touch and is always cramped. The charity does not mind losing people to other jobs and sees itself as naturally driven by the challenges associated with the work and the low pay of the sector. Many people leave reporting burnout because of the high work and cognitive load, the unreasonable expectations and the burning desire to help the beneficiaries. It is unlikely the organisation believes that the culture of CARING is the issue; instead, they will attribute burnout and high turnover to more tangible things such as the pay or the meaningfulness of the job itself (which is incorrect because, in fact, employees enjoy and find their roles meaningful).

An organisational culture that hampers wellbeing is not always a problem in terms of non-wellbeing indicators such as productivity or workflow. Organisational culture can certainly drive employee retention[1] and performance in general.[2] And a significant part of the differences in operational productivity within an industry have been attributed to culture.[3] However, a poor *wellbeing* organisational culture will ultimately be unsustainable and inevitably productivity will fall.

Values that promote wellbeing

If culture drives expectations and behaviours that affect wellbeing (for good or ill), what sort of organisational culture is needed for wellbeing to be nurtured?

To answer this question, let's look at some of the positive wellbeing values already identified. For example, good work–life boundaries; the ability to distinguish your personal life from your professional life, and thus your ability to disconnect from your work; the recognition and need for self-care and mutual care as definitive drivers of wellbeing; and the importance of wellbeing issues being addressed rather than brushed under the carpet.

There are three core pillars on which such a culture of wellbeing is built.

Pillar 1. From "I matter" to "we matter"

The first pillar is about encouraging people to look after themselves. Their work is essential, but they are ultimately more important than their work: the "I" matters. Sometimes individuals get so engrossed in work, because of its impact, its status and prestige, its salary, that any emotional and physical needs beyond these come second. This happens when work is a central part of someone's life and identity, and when they are strongly attached to an organisation. This kind of engagement is great. But the organisation also has a role to play in reminding its people why they should matter to themselves. By doing so, healthy work–life boundaries and self-care are encouraged.

But for organisations to appreciate and acknowledge people's work and contribution, the "I matter" needs to become "we matter". Putting yourself first means also paying attention to others, ensuring they feel recognised and heard, and that they are able to value themselves. When workers feel like their efforts amount to nothing, or do not move the needle forward, it reinforces their sense of being overwhelmed and a tendency to neglect themselves. For example, a study of organisational culture in the nursing profession found that the most effective cultures are those that give nurses a sense of personal accomplishment: when they felt they mattered, they were less likely to burn out.[4]

Pillar 2. Mental health matters

The second pillar is based on the phrase "mental health matters". Under this umbrella expression is the need for mental health to be visible and accepted. When organisations promote a culture of "mental health matters", people feel enabled to talk about mental health more openly. For many, mental health is still "not a thing". It can easily be stigmatised, with people suffering from depression and anxiety being socially excluded. This is no longer acceptable and organisations need to make it clear that this kind of thinking is at odds with organisational values. When visibility and acceptance of mental health are presented as a core value of the organisation, self-care is encouraged, and people suffering from mental health issues are more likely to find the support they need.

Pillar 3. Bend don't break

The third cultural element is the reminder that, pushed too far, people might become unable to work at all. We label it "Bend don't break": taking a break from work, or creating distance from a difficult and overwhelming situation (or asking someone to do so), is often preferable and necessary for longer-term health. When thinking about work, sustainable healthy practices are crucial to avoiding burnout and fatigue. The idea of wellbeing "breaks" is helpful whether you're managing yourself or others, and when setting boundaries around your professional life.

Those cultural pillars are only some examples of what would constitute a culture that supports wellbeing. By paying attention to those principles wellbeing-intelligent organisations can make these values more explicit, and part of everyday work life.

Language and wellbeing culture: why "therapy speak" matters

On their own, the values embedded in those cultural pillars may not be enough to create a wellbeing culture in organisations. Language matters too. The Let's Talk campaign, which encourages people to start conversations about mental health, illustrates the importance of a common language around mental health to break the stigma surrounding poor wellbeing. One of the projects associated with Let's Talk consisted of an outdoor photography exhibition in Regent's Place in London in 2019.[5] The photos displayed were portraits of people with their mental health challenges written on their faces.

Not every application of the Let's Talk campaign requires such radical engagement. The founding idea is to encourage people to feel more comfortable talking openly about their experiences of mental health. This effort was emulated by multiple organisations and workplaces including the *Sun* newspaper in the UK and the Canadian telecommunications company Bell. After a large-scale social media Let's Talk campaign coordinated by Bell in Ontario, researchers found there was rise in the number of visits to mental health services in the province.[6] Although many campaigns were aimed at the general public, some workplaces such as the Civil Service in the UK focused on changing the mindset within their organisation;

they used their own internal Let's Talk campaign to normalise conversations about mental health.

For people to be able to share their mental health experiences, they need the language to do so. Vocabularies, words and their definitions, as they become used and understood in the workplace, are part of the culture: they refer to experiences that are broadly understood. Even approachable and informed leaders and managers who play a role in providing awareness for mental health challenges need to be able to rely on a common language to do so. Some of the terms and their definitions explored in Part 1, about stress, anxiety, burnout and depression, and how they manifest themselves, are a useful starting point.

Other terms that are often negatively labelled as "therapy speak" can be useful for people to talk about their mental health. For example, clear boundaries between work and personal life matter to wellbeing. The term can be a powerful tool for people to signal when they are overloaded or overwhelmed and dragged in different directions. Another useful word to signal a potentially difficult situation is "triggered": someone might refuse to work in a situation that evokes a personal trauma, for example. By expressing the fear of being triggered, people can anticipate and ask to avoid a situation that might upset them. Those words are not an alternative to explaining why someone may feel triggered or their boundaries threatened, but while people might not always feel like sharing past experiences, they still might want to justify their reactions. It is not about avoiding emotions but conveying them to others to protect yourself.

At the opposite end of the spectrum, organisations need to be particularly aware of words that are used in a negative way and contribute to the stigmatising of mental health: "John is mental!" "The boss is being so schizophrenic." Language like this can have a devastating effect on people who might be experiencing genuine mental health challenges.

Because of the invisibility of wellbeing issues, it's easy to ignore them unless they are brought to the surface by the people who experience them. By developing and sharing vocabularies of wellbeing, it's possible to create a platform to understand and support each other better.

Towards a wellbeing-intelligent organisational culture

Not all organisational cultures are naturally attuned to wellbeing intelligence, as the example of Cynthia shows. In fact, for most people, workplaces are places of work, as the word indicates. They are not seen as appropriate spaces for people to share their emotions and get mental health support. Sometimes, organisational culture can actively *harm* wellbeing. If underlying values are at odds with self-care and mutual care (in the case of CARING, a focus on beneficiaries to the detriment of employees), wellbeing might be very low on the list of collective and individual priorities.

One such example is the tale of Pamela, a junior analyst who recently joined the investment banking industry. The expectation is that she should work as long as needed, even into the early hours of the morning, so she is often the last to leave the office. Pamela has been told that this is normal, and many of the senior analysts did the same thing when they joined. This culture of overwork has developed progressively and has become widely acceptable and part of the organisational culture: the "survivors" of investment banking often see this as a badge of honour, they lived to tell the tale, so others should too. This culture is reproduced through unspoken expectations that people should stay at their desks. People who do not conform to those tacit rules are likely to be excluded and struggle to be considered for promotion or opportunities to raise their profile. Pamela doesn't want to rock the boat or miss out on any prospects so continues to conform to the organisational culture, even though it has the potential to undermine her wellbeing.

This is a typical cultural tale: the values and beliefs are that this work is so important and complex that it justifies limited sleep, even though this behaviour is not justified by the workload. It's difficult for organisations in this industry to build a culture of wellbeing when divergence from industry norms is challenging. Many other industries have similarly challenging cultures, from high-end restaurants to prestigious strategy consulting firms. Organisations within these sectors rarely feel like breaking those strong norms that are perceived as being integral to their success.

The fact is that many organisational norms can trigger wellbeing issues: for example, a strong norm of presenteeism even when employees are sick, the way feedback is provided, how managers communicate, and whether they communicate outside working hours. In most cases, the norms can be observed at an individual and team level, which rings the alarm bell to make an effort to shift those well-anchored practices to broader, organisational changes.

To tackle those harmful wellbeing norms and change the culture, organisations can consider three practical steps.

Identify negative norms and highlight their consequences

Collect qualitative and quantitative evidence on how norms generate wellbeing issues, either directly by causing stress or indirectly by how they can be potentially counter-productive by making people less effective, less productive and less motivated. For example, annual performance reviews can be an opportunity for employees to report on norms – like work interactions and perceptions or feedback and communication styles – that they might feel hamper their motivation and wellbeing. For example, if Pamela felt able to use her probation review meeting to share the difficulty in switching off from work when she is expected to be present long after her working hours, this information (anonymised or not) should be shared with people who are in a position to push for a meaningful cultural change.

Similarly, consider a common unspoken norm that it's unjustified for people to take sick leave for mental health issues. If people report this experience, awareness around the issue has been raised and the norm can potentially be challenged.

Unpack harmful norms

Norms are often justified by organisations. Justification may come from the benefits that people get from engaging with norms or the assumptions that others have about them. For example, the norm of Pamela working late has meant that her superiors see her as someone who can be relied on and isn't afraid to go the extra mile. She seems extra committed to the organisation. In this sense the unhelpful norm has been justified for Pamela because of the high esteem she derives from her colleagues. This reasoning and justification of norms needs to be considered and interrogated.

Pamela may also stay late because she finds a bond and some pride in a shared experience with her peers, increasing her sense of connection at work, the idea that "they are in it together". For a while, the group of junior analysts may start to feel superhuman, working long hours and building a sense of camaraderie. Ultimately, though, working with this norm is unsustainable and there are other ways to create shared experiences with peers that do not harm wellbeing in the same way.

Shift the norms

Changing negative norms might feel like the most challenging part once they are identified and debunked. The core tool that changemakers have in their portfolio is to incentivise engagement with new norms. If incentives do not work (and they often might not if norms are enforced through peers), more radical changes from the top are needed. For example, closing offices during weekends or late at night shuts off the opportunity to work unreasonably long working hours. Pamela and her peers may find it easier to leave on time if they know the office will be closed after a certain time and the expectation for them to stay is therefore heavily constrained.

Shifting the vocabulary about the negative perception of mental health sick days, and encouraging people to take days off for their mental wellbeing when they need to, is likely to shift perceptions more generally. Senior leaders acting as role models – whether in terms of long hours or sick days – will also help to shift unhelpful norms.

Identifying problematic norms, debunking the rationales and assumptions behind them, and incentivising new norms, can contribute to shifting an organisational culture towards improved wellbeing.

Hybrid working and wellbeing culture

While the precise forms of hybrid and remote work will evolve in workplaces over the years, it is likely to become a new norm: compared with the pre-pandemic years, we will continue to balance the benefits of spending some of our working lives at home. Flexible working patterns due to hybrid working help people fit work around their personal lives, and the responsibilities they have (from caring for elder parents or children, to community roles). Research has found that the option of working from home reduces quit rates by 35% and that employees are ready to trade up to 10% of their salaries in exchange of working from home two or three days a week.[7] There are clear benefits for wellbeing, provided by the flexibility and the ability to focus in the home environment. And as most organisations have learnt how to make the most of working from home, it would be a pity not to capitalise on this revolution.

Although it can be harder to unplug from work when working from home, the ways in which people take breaks and use their time away from work has shifted to promote wellbeing.

For example:

- taking a break for a walk; stretching; desk yoga
- lunch away from the desk (which encourages better physical health)
- using breaks to get ahead of household chores so free time after work is maximised
- more conscious effort to unplug and put in boundaries; managers can lead by promoting boundaries and expectations.

Thanks to hybrid working, people are better able to choose their work environment and switch environment depending on their mood and the needs of the work they are doing. Neurodiverse workers in particular may find it easier to focus in certain environments and hybrid working allows this difference to be explored.

Let's take the example of Felix who has been diagnosed with attention deficit hyperactivity disorder (ADHD). He managed well growing up and at school. But in his new job, he works in a large open-plan office with many distractions. He is worried about how he will focus. His ability to work three days from home, however, helps him focus on deep work, and when he returns to the office every Wednesday, he can socialise with colleagues in his team and beyond. It has felt progressively more comfortable and he accepts he will do different types of work when at home and in the office.

Hybrid working does not only benefit those who are neurodiverse. Everyone will have a preferred working environment, which may change from week to week, but having flexible working as a cultural norm means that people feel more in control of their work. It gives them a sense of agency and flexibility that contributes to positive wellbeing.

But it's not all plain sailing. There are, of course, wellbeing risks associated with remote and hybrid working.[8] We will now look at the main culprits.

"Always on" culture

Hybrid working can make it more difficult to unplug completely from work, and people can feel more constantly on call than ever before. The difficulties in staying away from work are accentuated by the spread of digital technologies and communications (e.g. Teams, Slack and other messaging applications). By letting themselves slide into constant availability ("because work is too important!"), employees deprive themselves of the chance to refresh and recuperate away from colleagues and work.

There is increasing competition for workers' time. People are expected to meet growing demands in organisations, because technologies on which work is based change quickly. Notably, some of those demands also arise from the new world of work: for example, the number of meetings has increased, especially where there is the need for coordination and collaboration across locations.[9] Consequently, many people feel they are losing control over their time. Naturally, this pressure for time makes those employees scrambling for time more stressed, and more inclined to work extra hours at the expense of their personal lives.

The way in which work is structured and organised to avoid those pitfalls while capitalising on the new flexible modes of work is partly a question of culture. Addressing this question is crucial to wellbeing. The underlying values, beliefs and practices anchored in the life of organisations need to be thoroughly understood.

Presenteeism

Because hybrid or remote work is no longer confined to one physical space, it is possible to work anywhere and everywhere. But although space might no longer be a work boundary ("If I am not in the office, I can't help"), time still is: in this sense, it is crucial to respect people's time off in the evenings or at weekends.

Dangerous assumptions about presenteeism cause another fear: studies suggest that those who are not physically present in the office to interact with their colleagues are not as well recognised for their contributions.[10] People become naturally afraid not to show up at work, and thus force themselves to go into the office even when not mandated and not needed, sometimes at the expense of their productivity. Workers are becoming progressively more like the investment bankers who paradoxically stay late into the night despite the absence of a work task. Managers and organisational leaders need to eliminate this presenteeism bias so that their hybrid working policy can be accessible to everybody without fear of being judged for not showing up in the office.

Meeting norms

Another essential part of the culture on which wellbeing depends are the norms around meetings. During the covid pandemic, the number of meetings increased drastically to enable collaboration in a remote context. Many organisations are still stuck with a large number of meetings that are not useful.[11]

Meetings are not all bad for wellbeing. They can play a huge role in helping people connect with each other and feel embedded in their work community. They can help people address thorny issues and be creative together. Yet meetings need to have a clear purpose, involve the right people, and enable all voices to be expressed. A healthy number of meetings will generate a sense of belonging, leaving people time and space to focus on fulfilling their work duties.

Hybrid working is not all bad or all good for wellbeing. But regardless of the specifics it will inevitably affect how people feel about their work and each individual will have a preferred balance. It requires trial and error to see what works for each organisation, team and individual.

Diversity and a culture of wellbeing

A large body of research shows that under-represented groups are more likely to be exposed to bullying or harassment at work, which inevitably and drastically affects their wellbeing. Ethnic and sexual minorities, women and those with disabilities are disproportionately affected by workplace violence. Surveys of the National Health Service in England found that a third of minority ethnic staff had faced harassment.[12] US data suggest that almost half of LGBTQ+ workers have experienced unfair treatment at work.[13] Workplace sexual harassment has been found to trigger anxiety, depression and post-traumatic disorder.[14]

Less obviously, some demographics are also simply more likely to be exposed to mental health challenges and be less satisfied with their work.[15] Under-represented employees often feel their voices are not heard: there is a negative wellbeing effect, whether the belief is legitimate or not. Similarly, they may feel and sometimes do not get the same career progression opportunities or are not adequately recognised for their achievements. They may involuntarily lack visibility because of biases within their organisation or because they voluntarily avoid exposure. For example, research into LGBTQ+ employees suggests that they may voluntarily try to stay under the radar at work to avoid having to reveal their sexual identity, with implications for their anxiety and stress level, but also for recognition and advancement.[16]

In this sense, a comprehensive approach to workplace diversity is a central element of cultures that support wellbeing. Organisations need to actively protect under-represented groups from poor treatment that can affect their wellbeing. Organisations also need to work on inclusion and to help others feel comfortable in the workplace, so they can express themselves and how they feel about their wellbeing more openly. Diversity policies need to acknowledge how wellbeing hurdles might deprive an organisation of diverse talent.

Like any aspect of organisational culture, connecting core values and practice is crucial. The core values of a culture that fosters diversity revolve around openness, representation and inclusion, the ability to recognise and celebrate difference. Commitment to those values must be visible at all levels of the organisation, and translated into everyday practices such as hiring, promotion and communication. Policies should protect minorities from being marginalised, harassed or discriminated against. There should be an awareness of (and training in) anchored yet dangerous unconscious biases that may be present in organisations. Representations of organisational culture, like websites or promotion, should be inclusive and celebrate diversity in all its forms.

A culture of mentorship support can also help. Employee resource groups can offer a forum for people from a minority background to express their views, share their experiences and potentially take action together. Mentorship can also provide positive role models that are representative of a diverse organisational population.

On their own, though, these initiatives are often insufficient to tackle persistent disparities in how minorities access and benefit from mental health care.[17] They might fear not being understood because of cultural and identity differences (and because colleagues from a majority background might struggle to understand their experience). Responsiveness to wellbeing issues must be culturally sensitive. For example, experiences of sexual harassment in the workplace are often misunderstood. In our research on LGBTQ+ auditors, we found that gay men usually avoided reporting cases of harassment because they felt it would reveal their sexuality and they would not be believed.[18] In some cases, it triggered vicious cycles of anxiety and stress in work situations.

It is crucial for any wellbeing-intelligent organisation to consider the treatment of its most diverse employees. Are they fully understood? Will there be empathy and effort to understand their everyday experience? What might disproportionately affect their wellbeing? Are policies, practices and managerial approaches adapted to them? Mapping out what might make them feel uncomfortable, at odds with the culture or excluded will help to level the playing field and ensure that diverse employees receive the support they deserve.

For good or ill, organisational culture influences work environments, relationships, expectations, communication – and wellbeing. Solid wellbeing cultures depend on understanding and mitigating harmful or unhelpful cultural values and norms.

Some harmful norms might revolve around working modes, meetings or diversity-related biases, and understanding and mapping these norms is the first step towards positive wellbeing changes. For example, a work culture that values work–life balance (for example, by ensuring that people take their annual leave) will have a range of positive wellbeing implications. Positive changes around wellbeing, and how people talk about it in organisations, requires a common language and a workplace culture that fosters open communication, ultimately alleviating the stigma around mental health.

When thinking about wellbeing and organisational culture, there is a tendency to focus on the negative – for example, rooting out toxic cultures. But working towards positive cultures in the ways described in this chapter has huge potential to preserve wellbeing, morale and job satisfaction, all factors that underpin organisational success.

10

Wellbeing strategies, policies and support

Salesforce, a US company that provides cloud-based software for managing customer relationships, has built an inspirational wellbeing strategy; the practices it has put in place are aligned with the core pillars of its organisational culture. The company's culture relies on the concept of *'Ohana* (the Hawaiian word for "family"): employees are responsible for each other, and mutual care and trust are central to work interactions. The Salesforce wellbeing offering is aligned with this culture. Like many other firms, it offers counselling and dedicated mental health coaching, but, in the spirit of care, it also provides preventive mental health support and interactive workshops. The aim is to tackle wellbeing before it becomes an issue because it is perceived as the collective responsibility of everyone in the organisation. To tie everything together, and to signpost the support available, Salesforce has been running town halls dedicated to mental health since 2021.

What Salesforce demonstrates is that even the most positive and supportive organisational culture – its values, the assumptions and beliefs – is not enough on its own to create wellbeing-intelligent organisations. The culture also needs to translate into concrete practices. Together, those concrete practices need to constitute a holistic wellbeing strategy.

Unfortunately, many organisational wellbeing strategies fall short. Policies and wellbeing benefits are often ill adapted and not fit for purpose. For example, we know of a police organisation that provides an online counselling service through an outsourced provider. Although the offer of counselling is well intended, the provider has little or no idea about the daily work and experience of police officers, and therefore the specific stresses, anxieties and even trauma associated with policing are not understood. It's a case of the right idea (providing counselling) but poor implementation (failing to see that support needs to be more focused and tailored to the need).

Even when policies and benefits are adapted to the context, they might be inconsistent and incoherent as an overall wellbeing strategy. One practice might clash with another, making apparent some fundamental issue in how wellbeing is addressed. This might lead to the claim that the organisation is not serious about wellbeing. For example, offering unlimited holiday can be a double-edged sword, leaving more engaged workers to take over the load left by their less engaged colleagues. In companies with high pressure to perform and limited opportunities for delegation, people feel unable to take time off, and the unlimited holiday policy is therefore pointless. Wellness programmes (such as the mental health coaching and workshops offered at Salesforce) are likely to be ignored if people are unable or unwilling to find the time to access them. An even more apparent clash can be found in organisations that promote a digital detox in an effort to reduce screen time, but offer online therapies as part of the same wellbeing provision. Although both useful and necessary in isolation, when placed together in the same wellbeing strategy, the two initiatives are no longer complementary.

The core policies and practices that make up a wellbeing-intelligent workplace need to be part of a coherent organisational-level wellbeing strategy. There needs to be consistency in approach towards wellbeing and practices need to be relevant, directly targeting the wellbeing challenges experienced by employees. With this core in place, organisations are better equipped to understand where to allocate investments in wellbeing support. A clear coherent strategy can also direct what services and provisions are most needed in the organisation, and how these provisions align with policy to create synergies across different forms of support.

Mental health and wellbeing policy

Most organisations will want to set up a mental health and wellbeing policy to underpin their practice. A mental health and wellbeing policy is there to make a statement and serve as a commitment to the employees and other stakeholders on the question of wellbeing. A good policy would recognise upfront the importance of mental health and wellbeing, both because it is the right thing to do and because it contributes to the success of the organisation and its employees.

Typically, a mental health and wellbeing policy would include:

- an overarching statement of intent (answering the questions "Why is wellbeing important to us as an organisation?" and "What is wellbeing for us?")
- key principles (e.g. around work–life balance, the right to disconnect, and the recognition of mental health as an important factor for success)
- employer/employee responsibility (e.g. what falls on the employer to be addressed, and what requires the employee to seek help outside the organisation)

- how the policy will be implemented (e.g. what wellbeing programmes are due to be set up, mental health provision and support, and its assessment).

The very existence of the policy can also help to combat the stigma around mental health and normalise wellbeing issues. A mental health and wellbeing policy is also a good way to codify the organisational culture; it can restate the principles and values on which the organisation is built. This might be as simple as highlighting a strict position against harassment or discrimination. But it should also include norms such as the importance of taking time off, trust and work relationships.

The policy can also state how the wellbeing strategy will be set up, who will contribute to designing it, who will decide what to set up and what to invest in, and how support programmes and wellbeing practices will be assessed. To make this happen, organisations can consider having a committee made of various employee groups. Such a steering group can ensure the coherence of the strategy, its alignment with the policy, and assess needs on a regular basis.

A wellbeing policy, of course, is only as good as the concrete practices that the organisation puts in place to make it a reality. A coherent wellbeing strategy must ensure that there are no blind spots upstream (before wellbeing becomes an issue) or downstream (to address wellbeing issues once they have arisen), providing organisations with a holistic perspective.

The sieve model

The sieve model of organisational wellbeing strategies is a tool to help organisations take this holistic approach to wellbeing.[1] The model acknowledges three steps to addressing wellbeing as an organisation:

1. pre-empt issues
2. detect who is affected
3. remedy issues when they have become unavoidable.

Each step includes core practices and approaches for achieving wellbeing goals at each stage.

The clue to the model is in the name. The aim is to create a filter to address wellbeing issues before they become critical, either when they are more manageable or sometimes even before they happen. The sieve metaphor is also about recognising that some mental health challenges are inevitable, no matter how good your strategy – for example, heightened levels of anxiety due to a challenging business environment. But having a strategy in place will help you spot these challenges from afar, anticipating when anxiety is likely to be heightened and preparing for it.

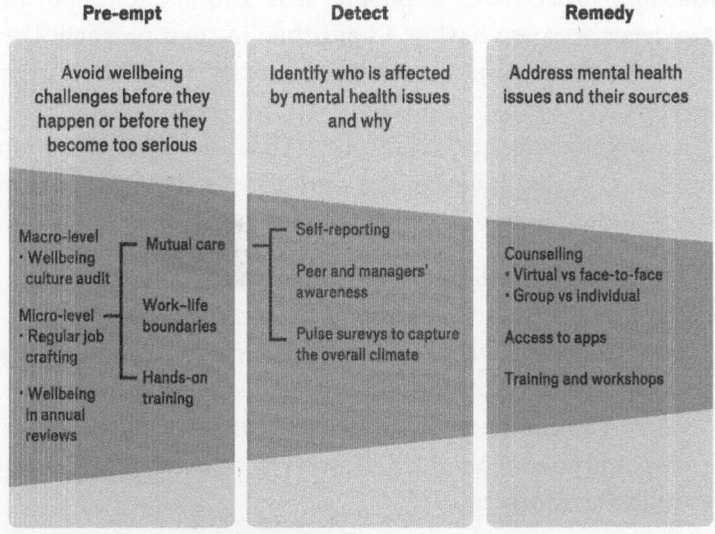

Figure 15: **The sieve model**

Similarly, issues in people's personal lives are likely to spill over into their work: the mental health consequences of these issues may not be avoidable but, with the right strategies in place, they can be detected and acknowledged earlier. The upstream part of the model (pre-empt) is as much about more minor issues as it is about tackling more intangible workplace culture problems.

Figure 15 on the previous page summarises the sieve model for addressing wellbeing issues at work, and each of the steps is explored in the following sections of this chapter.

Pre-empting wellbeing issues

The failure to pre-empt mental health issues at work is an organisational fault, which is why organisations need to care deeply about what they can do to tackle them before they occur or get worse. Pre-empting is about anticipating and mitigating what may cause harm to people. It is also about supporting employees who are having a hard time in their personal lives and might need support when those challenges spill over in the workplace.

An organisational culture of care can help pre-empt and address wellbeing issues in the workplace, adopting a positive organisational culture that requires a focus on two key outcomes.

- **Work–life boundaries**. Even the most passionate employees need to have a solid sense of where and how work stops, and where their personal life starts. This allows employees to be able to recharge and step away from work. A strong sense of work–life boundaries can pre-empt burnout or heightened stress, acting as a protective wellbeing measure.

- **Mutual care.** Employees should care about each other, and be aware of what others are experiencing in their personal or professional lives, and how it affects their interactions and performance at work. Mutual care is as much about awareness as about taking supportive actions and designing an organisation that puts people's wellbeing on the radar. Increasing this awareness means that employees with stress or anxiety are more likely to be spotted and supported.

There are two sets of concrete practices that can help make these outcomes a reality on the ground.

Wellbeing culture audit

A wellbeing culture audit is a thorough examination of the core values, assumptions and norms underpinning an organisation's behaviours. It focuses on the values, beliefs and norms affecting wellbeing, scanning for practices that potentially prevent wellbeing because of a failure of mutual care or erosion of work–life boundaries. It can address a simple question: is this practice risky for wellbeing? Or it might look at wellbeing risks and trace them back to a specific practice.

Here's how an audit might work.

1. Survey all employees to get a sense of wellbeing. This can be via pulse surveys, open-ended feedback, or reports via one-to-one meetings and wellbeing agendas.

2. Incorporate data on workplace engagement. This will include the number of sick days taken and mental health days. The rate of turnover and employee exit interview data can feed into this.

3. Consider the strength of typical work practices, policies

and assumptions in your organisation and how they promote work–life boundaries and mutual care.

4. Connect the positive and negative aspects of your culture identified in previous steps with actual practice and set up a plan to change those practices. For example, if people tend to work at weekends, consider preventing access to your servers on Sundays.

5. Once again, survey all employees in the following months to observe whether the change in practice has had concrete positive implications, or has led to problems elsewhere. For example, if people have switched from weekend to night-time working, a deeper change is needed to re-examine workload and expectations.

The steps above aim to encourage mindful wellbeing practices which can ultimately influence the organisation's culture.

The wellbeing culture audit is also there to improve existing approaches. What can you change or add to enhance current wellbeing practices? What other initiatives might you try? For example, giving employees the time to socialise and get to know each other for reasons other than work will support trust and encourage mutual care. So you could consider setting up a coffee morning every week where people can unwind and see the friends they have made at work. Or you could encourage collaboration with people in other departments to build relationships across teams.

While the wellbeing culture audit takes a broad view on improving an organisation's approach to wellbeing, it is crucial to use its results to set up practices at a micro level to support routine and daily interactions.

Job design assessments

Poorly crafted jobs with too many tasks can lead to burnout. When you allocate a job, you assume a given workload. But often these assumptions need to change. Imagine hiring for a fast-expanding start-up or an organisation that has to shift its activity regularly because of its changing context. For example, during covid, teachers had to teach and be IT specialists, as they had to learn about a range of new technologies and support. An office manager in a start-up might see their role expanding daily. Often, though, an organisation might take time to realise it needs to change what people do or hire more people, or it might be reluctant to do so because of a lack of resources.

In the meantime, jobs that might previously have given people enough time and headspace to do their work suddenly become overwhelming. This is why organisations should carry out *regular job design assessments*. This involves mapping out the time needed for tasks to understand whether you need to adapt capacity – for example, passing on some tasks to others or hiring more people. Regular job design assessments can also help under-used employees who might feel depressed or stuck in their role; people can be consulted on what more they might want to learn, and how they see their portfolio of activities growing.

Re-assessments can occur at an employee's request, or at a frequency adapted to the organisation's activity – for example, every few months if changes affect jobs regularly or if new activities are added frequently.

Wellbeing and regular reviews

Pre-empting for wellbeing issues should also be part of regular reviews, like one-to-ones and annual reviews and evaluations (as described in Chapter 6). Annual reviews can include wellbeing goals around work–life balance – for example, making sure that people take all their annual leave and are not reading work emails after hours. They are also an opportunity to review job design and work arrangements, such as more flexible working for caring responsibilities.

Detecting wellbeing issues

The second step of the sieve model is to detect who is affected by wellbeing issues. Some of what we have explored to pre-empt wellbeing issues will also help detect them when they arise. Better mutual awareness and care will enable people to detect more easily when their colleagues or peers are suffering.

But many people experience stress and anxiety without it being visible even to the most wellbeing-intelligent colleague until how they feel has spiralled into burnout and absence. So an organisational culture that renders wellbeing issues visible and destigmatises them is also crucial. If stigma is alleviated, individuals are more likely to talk openly about their challenges with colleagues who can support them directly.

Let's take the example of Margot, a senior partner in a boutique consulting firm. Margot has been noticeably short-tempered in the last few weeks and has struggled to stay on top of her work. She is in the process of adopting a child and the uncertainty is weighing on her. She has not taken time off as she has been waiting for the court order to come through before she starts her adoption leave.

Fortunately, Margot has been comfortable enough to talk about her journey to close colleagues, including other partners in the firm as well as more junior staff who have had to suffer her short fuse. These allies know enough about Margot's situation to realise that her behaviour is not who she is, but a result of what she is experiencing in her personal life. Importantly,

Margot can also acknowledge that her life is spilling over into her work.

When someone at the top reveals how their mental health might be affecting their leadership and communication skills, they convey the message that it is okay to have a bad day at work, and that personal difficulties can inevitably impact your work. This is not about people making excuses for themselves but instead trying to provide tools for others to exercise empathy and disentangle what is a working or managerial style and what is the effect of a stressful personal moment. Such role modelling makes people feel more comfortable talking about mental health. And importantly, people will be more sensitive about how mental health might affect their colleagues.

Wellbeing leads

Wellbeing leads promote mental health awareness and training and act as sounding boards for people to talk to about the issues they are facing. They are often volunteers, but they can also be selected by the organisations for their listening skills. They need to be given training and a clear scope and framework for their role. For example, wellbeing leads would not be expected to counsel colleagues, but they may be expected to signpost appropriate support and offer a listening ear. Many people acting as wellbeing leads have themselves experienced mental health issues, and have built a helpful sensitivity around their own experience.

Pulse surveys and focus groups

Beyond encouraging people to self-report their challenges at work, it is crucial to set up organisational-level initiatives to detect mental health issues. Most commonly, organisations use pulse surveys to capture how people are feeling about their work.

Pulse surveys are short (no more than ten questions) and can be taken in just a few minutes. Questions can include simple yes/no responses (e.g. do you take your lunch breaks?), involve scales to understand the extent of an issue (e.g. on a scale of 1 to 5, how satisfied are you with your role?), or can be open questions that encourage feedback. Administering surveys after an online meeting or as people start their day can help organisations transform survey-taking into a more routine activity. Whether those surveys are kept anonymous or not is a question of trade-offs. Participants could be asked to provide their identity on the condition that this information is accessible only to a handful of people, such as HR. However, anonymity is more likely to get honest responses. As a compromise, participants could be asked to provide other general demographic information, such as area of operations, the unit or team they work with, or details such as job title, gender or age.

One simple question can go a long way in detecting mental health challenges.

How often have you felt stressed or overwhelmed at work in the last two weeks?

Using a specific time frame (e.g. the last two weeks) is useful to understand changes as you collect more than one wave of survey response. Feedback on matters like job satisfaction, relationship with colleagues, recognition, belonging to the organisation and development opportunities provides an important insight into the potential causes of mental health difficulties.

Possible questions to ask include:

- Do you feel your managers support your work and your career development adequately? (to unpack relationships with management)

- Do you feel your team collaborates effectively? (to look at team-level issues)
- Do you feel proud to work for your organisation? Do you feel aligned with your organisation's values? (to test identification)
- Do you feel recognised for your work? (for recognition)
- Do you feel you are growing and developing at work? (for personal growth)
- Do you feel you have enough autonomy in conducting your work tasks? (to look at autonomy, which is an essential driver of motivation)

You could also include other questions to explore specific issues.

To capture thoughts on potential burnout, ask:

- How confident have you been in coping with work-related challenges in the last two weeks?
- How well do you disconnect from work when you finish your day or are on holiday?
- How do you relax when you are not at work?

To identify whether people feel psychological safety with regards to mental health, ask:

- How often do you seek help or support for your mental health at work?
- How comfortable are you to talk about mental health?
- At work, do you know who to ask for wellbeing help?

The data produced by pulse surveys can be combined with tangible measures such as turnover rates or sick days to provide a clearer picture of wellbeing issues in the organisation. Hard data like this can provide momentum and justification for action but also might present an aspect that would otherwise be ignored: employees might not report low mental health but leave the organisation in droves, or take a large number of sick days. This might signal that employees do not feel comfortable recognising their mental health challenges. Despite these issues, pulse surveys are a versatile tool to help you draw a heatmap of mental health issues within your organisation (i.e. a cartography of what parts of the organisation, what departments or teams, are most affected by mental health issues) and what might be causing them.

Results can be explored more qualitatively in follow-up *focus groups*. When an organisation wants to explore a specific aspect of its wellbeing strategy, whether it is a positive aspect (e.g. fostering a positive organisational culture, shaping the organisation's purpose) or a more negative one (e.g. dealing with conflict and difficult conversations, dealing with prejudice and bias), they can draw together a group of people to discuss it. Focus groups can be guided by a moderator who will kickstart the discussion with a question (e.g. What is distinctive about our organisation? How do you feel we deal with conflict in our organisation?) and lead the conversation that follows.

Detecting wellbeing issues is an essential step of the sieve model. The challenge is to give visibility to problems that are usually repressed. If issues are not detected, they might not be addressed; they might get worse over time, and stress and anxiety could spread throughout the organisation. But giving visibility to mental health issues is also about breaking the barriers around those who suffer from them, and normalising them: if someone believes they are the only person to suffer stress and anxiety, they are likely to isolate themselves. The recognition that mental health issues are affecting many in the workplace is helpful for people not only to care and support each other, but also to address the problem collectively.

Remedying wellbeing issues

Identifying the causes of mental health issues is crucial to the pre-empting and detecting steps of the sieve model. As we have seen, mutual care and balanced work–life boundaries can enable wellbeing-intelligent individuals to pre-empt mental health issues. In the detecting step, focus groups and pulse surveys will help locate in which part of the organisation mental health issues are most present, and what might be causing them.

With this diagnosis in hand, you can design a strategy to remedy the wellbeing problems you have uncovered. Problems of workload and feelings of being overwhelmed can be addressed by an analysis of job and task design. Work–life boundaries can be improved by setting clear rules for people to disconnect from their work: no email on their personal phone, for example. Approaching those issues together rather than separately is crucial. For example, a "no emails during the weekend" policy can be set up in organisations that are concerned with the mental health cost of overwork. But employees might still feel pressurised for time and emailing out of office hours might be symptom of a more general overload. In this case, revisiting the tasks attached to each job and considering reallocating the tasks or even hiring more people might be the solution. Similarly, flexible working arrangements (for example, letting employees work four extended days a week, or work on a Saturday instead of a Wednesday) may alleviate the pressures related to caring for dependants, provided that similar accommodations are made available to others too.

The pre-empting and detecting stages won't necessarily help employees struggling with difficult times in their personal lives.

Yet their personal difficulties will affect their ability to work. Setting up a provision to help those employees will also benefit those who have issues caused directly by work. The truth is that employees who identify work as the source of their worries are often experiencing work–life interference effect: they might be struggling with work tasks because of personal challenges.

Access to counselling

Remedying will frequently involve setting up access to counselling services. Counselling can take many shapes: on a virtual platform or face to face, in a group or individually. Group counselling is used in many large organisations to help employees deal with events that affect a large part of the workforce: the death of a colleague, a merger or acquisition, or a significant change project. In this case, group counselling is useful because it helps people share their views and feelings and address isolation and a common-knowledge problem. Individual counselling is more suitable when the problems are specific to an individual.

Counselling provisions (whether virtual or face to face) can be outsourced or offered in-house. The advantage of developing in-house capacity is that your counsellor will quickly understand what your employees are experiencing at work, what is typically a source of stress and anxiety, and the best way to address these issues. The disadvantage is that you do not have much flexibility if demand increases, and employees might be concerned about anonymity. An alternative is to build relationships with a dedicated set of counsellors working for an external provider. Those counsellors can develop a precise understanding of your employees' needs while also providing extra capacity as needed.

Other resources can be outsourced: for example, employees can be given access to meditation and mental health apps (such as Calm or Headspace) that provide guided meditation, podcasts, stories to fall asleep to and other resources that can help employees. More specialised apps are also often available: for example, LinkedIn provides its employees with Sleepio, an app to help those struggling with sleep.

Mental health training

Mental health training will help people detect and address wellbeing challenges. For example, the insurance company AXA offers a range of programmes to its clients, from learning how to work from home in the best physical conditions to more traditional stress management techniques.

The training needs to be about not only describing issues but also sharing skills like those in this book, including models to challenge negative maintenance cycles and connect behaviours with the drivers of those behaviours. Importantly, participants need to be put in practical situations (such as simulations or role play) to try those skills, understand their potential and learn how to use them.

Despite the potential of these services, whether workshops, training, apps or counselling, they are often ignored by employees. Data suggests that in the United States, 87% of firms have wellbeing programmes, but only 23% of people are using them.[2] This is the consequence of a lack of visibility for those programmes and the stigma around mental health issues. But it can also be due to employees doubting the potential of those programmes to improve their life, or about their relevance to their specific context. They might also perceive that they lack the time to engage with wellbeing programmes alongside a busy working life.

That's why it's important to be clear about the benefits of any services when publicising them. It needs to be obvious that the benefits are worth the investment of time: a struggling employee is likely to spend more time struggling to complete a task when unwell than if they take the time to attend to their wellbeing and then return to the task refreshed. Word of mouth is also important. Make the most of service users who have had positive experiences and are prepared to spread the word.

This chapter has explored how wellbeing intelligence can be translated into practices and policies at an organisational level. Those practices and policies need to constitute a coherent and holistic wellbeing strategy for the organisation and work alongside organisational cultures that destigmatise mental health, maintain work–life boundaries, and encourage mutual care.

There is no single way to set up a wellbeing-intelligent organisation, but there are many opportunities to set up a range of interventions and to test their effect. Experimentation might be necessary, but the rewards, as we have shown, are important for all three wellbeing circles.

Epilogue

Improving your workplace; developing wellbeing intelligence

It is now up to you, reader, to develop your wellbeing intelligence and take it to your workplace. In concluding this journey, we invite you to reflect on the circles of wellbeing intelligence – self, team and organisation – and to adopt the motto "Know yourself to help others and foster positive change."

As you navigate these circles, think about a workplace culture that prioritises understanding, empathy and positive behavioural shifts. By fostering open conversations and empowering individuals to take charge of their mental wellbeing, you will pave the way for a future where organisational success is intricately woven with the flourishing mental health of its members.

We predict that wellbeing intelligence will be not just a great asset but also a necessary workplace skill. But it's a skill that isn't innate or acquired instantly. It requires time, patience and a commitment to learning. As you navigate the complexities of the modern workplace, wellbeing intelligence will undoubtedly play a pivotal role in shaping the successful leaders of tomorrow.

That doesn't mean that we expect people at work to do the job of trained mental health professionals. Having clear boundaries around the levels of support that is appropriate to offer is essential. But we can all learn from the skills used by these professionals to build our wellbeing intelligence and provide sensitive and supportive mental health "first aid".

And that matters. This rapid evolution of the world of work is not without its challenges. People are increasingly expected to adapt to new technologies, navigate complex information landscapes, and manage relationships in diverse and dispersed teams. In the meantime, their organisations have to remain agile, adapt or die. These demands can place significant stress on employees, potentially leading to mental health issues such as anxiety and depression.

People may also experience challenges in their personal lives, especially in a world that can feel politically and economically unstable. These anxieties will inevitably spill over into the workplace.

In this context, mental health skills are becoming increasingly important. The expectation is that employers will support people's mental health, just as they would their physical health. Organisations that fail to meet these expectations risk damaging their reputation and their ability to attract and retain talent.

These skills include recognising signs of mental distress in yourself and others, managing stress effectively, and seeking help when needed – all crucial for maintaining a healthy and productive workforce. Organisations that invest in developing these skills are likely to see benefits in terms of increased productivity, reduced absenteeism, and improved employee engagement and retention.

But this won't happen on its own. There needs to be a proactive emphasis on wellbeing and a democratisation of wellbeing skills at work.

We hope that our book will contribute to this by offering

fresh perspectives for understanding, managing and promoting mental health wellbeing at work.

By equipping people with the right tools and skills and fostering a supportive and understanding work environment, everyone can build organisations that are places of wellbeing *and* productivity. A healthy dose of wellbeing intelligence will help you along the way.

Acknowledgements

We are grateful for the support of our family (in particular, Rajinder, Elisabeth, Gerard, Ruman and Nicolas) and friends. This work is also a testament to the living memory of our dog, Bruce, who did so much for our wellbeing, and Kiran's father, who instilled in her a profound love of books.

We are also indebted to our fantastic editor at Profile Books, Clare Grist Taylor, who helped us sharpen our points and drastically improve the quality of this work.

Notes

Introduction

1. According to a poll conducted by Vitality, half of home workers reported a higher productivity. Vitality, "Healthy hybrid working: building healthy workplaces in an evolving working world" (2022). www.vitality.co.uk/business/healthy-hybrid-report/
2. According to Gallup. D. Witters and S. Agrawal, "The economic cost of poor employee mental health", www.gallup.com (November 3rd 2022).
3. According to a 2023 CIPD survey of employers with regards to the statement "Employee wellbeing is on senior leaders' agendas". "Health and wellbeing at work", survey report, Chartered Institute of Personnel and Development, London (September 2023), p. 5.
4. B. Johnson, "Churchill wrote to keep the black dog of depression at bay", *Telegraph* (October 11th 2014).
5. C. Naylor et al., "Long-term conditions and mental health: the cost of co-morbidities", The King's Fund and Centre for Mental Health (February 2012).

Chapter 1: Wellbeing at work and why it matters

1. Adapted from M. Swarbrick, "A wellness approach to mental health recovery" in A. Rudnick (ed.), *Recovery of People with Mental Illness: Philosophical and Related Perspectives* (Oxford University Press, 2012).
2. World Health Organisation, Depression and Other Common Mental Disorders: Global Health Estimates (WHO, 2017).
3. Ibid.
4. B. Erdogan et al., "Whistle while you work: a review of the life satisfaction literature", *Journal of Management*, 38(4) (2012), pp. 1038–83.

5. S. Dattani, "What is the lifetime risk of depression?", Our World in Data (May 18th 2022).
6. World Health Organisation, "Anxiety disorders", fact sheet (September 27th 2023).
7. C. Baker and E. Kirk-Wade, "Mental health statistics: prevalence, services and funding in England", House of Commons Library (March 1st 2024).
8. S. McManus et al., "Mental health and wellbeing in England: the adult psychiatric morbidity survey 2014", NHS Digital (2016).
9. D. Stevenson and P. Farmer, "Thriving at work: a review of mental health and employers", Department for Work and Pensions & Department of Health and Social Care, London (October 26th 2017).
10. N. Bolger, A. Zuckerman and R.C. Kessler, "Invisible support and adjustment to stress", *Journal of Personality and Social Psychology*, 79(6) (2000), p. 953.
11. R. Burman and T.G. Goswami, "A systematic literature review of work stress", *International Journal of Management Studies*, 5(3–9) (2018), pp. 112–32.
12. A.H. Kemp and D.S. Quintana, "The relationship between mental and physical health: insights from the study of heart rate variability", *International Journal of Psychophysiology*, 89(3) (2013), pp. 288–96.
13. M.E. Clinton et al., "Lost control driving home: a dual-pathway model of self-control work demands and commuter driving", *Journal of Management*, 48(4) (2021), pp. 821–50.
14. G. Halkos and D. Bousinakis, "The effect of stress and satisfaction on productivity", *International Journal of Productivity and Performance Management*, 59(5) (2010), pp. 415–31.
15. J.M. Kensbock, L. Alkærsig and C. Lomberg, "The epidemic of mental disorders in business: how depression, anxiety, and stress spread across organisations through employee mobility", *Administrative Science Quarterly*, 67(1) (2022), pp. 1–48.
16. Poor mental health costs UK employers up to £45bn a year. "It pays to support mental health at work", Deloitte.com (2020).
17. Mental Health Taskforce to the NHS in England, "The five-year forward view for mental health" (February 2016).
18. Stevenson and Farmer, "Thriving at work: a review of mental health and employers".

19. Although evidence suggested that Maslow himself is not behind the hierarchy of needs, and that there is little empirical support for an escalation of needs. The approach nevertheless is a useful way to think about them. See T. Bridgman, S. Cummings and J.A. Ballard, "Who built Maslow's pyramid? A history of the creation of management studies' most famous symbol and its implications for management education", *Academy of Management Learning and Education*, 18(1) (2019), pp. 81–98.

Chapter 2: Four mental health challenges at work

1. See the Flash Eurobarometer – OSH Pulse survey 2022, European Agency for Safety and Health at Work. osha.europa.eu/en/facts-and-figures/osh-pulse-occupational-safety-and-health-post-pandemic-workplaces
2. T. Woo et al., "Global prevalence of burnout symptoms among nurses: a systematic review and meta-analysis", *Journal of Psychiatric Research*, 123 (2020), pp. 9–20.
3. Asana, "Anatomy of Work Special Report. The unexplored link between imposter syndrome and burnout", Asana (2022).
4. S.F. Javaid et al., "Epidemiology of anxiety disorders: global burden and sociodemographic associations", *Middle East Current Psychiatry*, 30(1) (2023), p. 44.
5. World Health Organisation, "Depressive disorder (depression)", fact sheet (March 31st 2023).
6. National Institute for Health and Care Excellence, "Depression in adults: treatment and management", NICE guideline NG222 (June 29th 2022).
7. A. Brabban and D. Turkington, "The search for meaning: detecting congruence between life events, underlying schema and psychotic symptoms" in A.P. Morrison (ed.), *A Casebook of Cognitive Therapy for Psychosis* (New York: Brunner-Routledge, 2002), pp. 59–75.

Chapter 3: Towards wellbeing intelligence

1. P. Salovey and J.D. Mayer, "Emotional intelligence", *Imagination, Cognition and Personality*, 9(3) (1990), pp. 185–211.
2. D. Goleman, *Emotional Intelligence: Why It Can Matter More Than IQ* (Bloomsbury, 1995, republished 2020).

Chapter 4: Assessing your own wellbeing

1. S. Subel, M. Stepanek and T. Roulet, "How shifts in remote behavior affect employee well-being", *MIT Sloan Management Review* (April 18th 2022).

2. K. Kroenke, R.L. Spitzer and J.B. Williams, "The PHQ-9: validity of a brief depression severity measure", *Journal of General Internal Medicine*, 16(9) (2001), pp. 606–13.

3. R.L. Spitzer et al., "A brief measure for assessing generalized anxiety disorder: the GAD-7", *Archives of Internal Medicine*, 166(10) (2006), pp. 1092–7.

4. D. Greenberger and C.A. Padesky, *Mind over Mood: A Cognitive Therapy Treatment Manual for Clients* (New York: Guilford Press, 1995).

5. J. Luft and H. Ingham, "The Johari window: a graphic model of interpersonal awareness", *Proceedings of the Western Training Laboratory in Group Development*, Los Angeles, University of California (1955).

Chapter 5: Tools for self-care

1. A.T. Beck (ed.), *Cognitive Therapy of Depression* (New York: Guilford Press, 1979).

2. C.B. Ferster, "A functional analysis of depression", *American Psychologist*, 28(10) (1973), p. 857.

3. T.D. Borkovec et al., "Stimulus control applications to the treatment of worry", *Behaviour Research and Therapy*, 21(3) (1983), pp. 247–51.

4. D.J. Good et al., "Contemplating mindfulness at work: an integrative review", *Journal of Management*, 42(1) (2016), pp. 114–42.

5. L. Guillaumie, O. Boiral and J. Champagne, "A mixed-methods systematic review of the effects of mindfulness on nurses", *Journal of Advanced Nursing*, 73(5) (2017), pp. 1017–34.

6. A. Kirca, J.M. Malouff and J. Meynadier, "The effect of expressed gratitude interventions on psychological wellbeing: a meta-analysis of randomised controlled studies", *International Journal of Applied Positive Psychology*, 8(1) (2023), pp. 63–86.

Chapter 6: Detecting mental health difficulties in others

1. A. Zamir, A. Tickle and R. Sabin-Farrell, "A systematic review of the evidence relating to disclosure of psychological distress by mental health professionals within the workplace", *Journal of Clinical Psychology*, 78(9) (2022), pp. 1712–38.
2. K.E. Toth et al., "Disclosure dilemmas: how people with a mental health condition perceive and manage disclosure at work", *Disability and Rehabilitation*, 44(25) (2022), pp. 7791–801.
3. National institute of Mental Health, "Ask suicide-screening questions (ASQ) toolkit". www.nimh.nih.gov/research/research-conducted-at-nimh/asq-toolkit-materials

Chapter 7: Wellbeing tools to support others

1. K.Y. Kim et al., "Supportive leadership and job performance: contributions of supportive climate, team-member exchange (TMX), and group-mean TMX", *Journal of Business Research*, 134 (2021), pp. 661–74.
2. According to Amy C. Edmondson. *The Fearless Organization: Creating Psychological Safety in the Workplace for Learning, Innovation and Growth* (New Jersey: Wiley, 2018).
3. McKinsey, "What is psychological safety?", www.mckinsey.com (July 17th 2023).
4. A. Gallo, "What is psychological safety?", *Harvard Business Review* (February 15th 2023).
5. R. O'Donovan and E. Mcauliffe, "A systematic review of factors that enable psychological safety in healthcare teams", *International Journal for Quality in Health Care*, 32(4) (2020), pp. 240–50.
6. C.R. Rogers, "The necessary and sufficient conditions of therapeutic personality change", *Journal of Consulting Psychology*, 21(2) (1957), p. 95.
7. R. Akhanemhe, S. Wallbank and N. Greenberg, "An evaluation of REACT mental health training for healthcare supervisors", *Occupational Medicine*, 71(3) (2021), pp. 127–30.
8. Mental Health First Aid/Skills Training Group, "ALGEE: 5-step MHFA Action Plan".
9. P. Jenkins, "Gerard Egan's skilled helper model", in S. Palmer and R. Woolfe (eds), *Integrative and Eclectic Counselling and Psychotherapy*

(London: Sage, 2000), pp. 163–80. Egan first described his approach in: G. Egan, *The Skilled Helper: A Model for Systematic Helping and Interpersonal Relating* (Thomson Brooks/Cole, 1975).

Chapter 8: Managing and leading with wellbeing intelligence

1. D. Joseph et al., "Is a happy leader a good leader? A meta-analytic investigation of leader trait affect and leadership", *Leadership Quarterly*, 26(4) (2015), pp. 557–76.

2. S.M. Carter and M.A. West, "Reflexivity, effectiveness and mental health in BBC-TV production teams", *Small Group Research*, 29(5) (1998), pp. 583–601.

3. G.S. van der Vegt and J.S. Bunderson, "Learning and performance in multidisciplinary teams: the importance of collective team identification", *Academy of Management Journal*, 48(3) (2005), pp. 532–47.

4. J. Skakon et al., "Are leaders' wellbeing, behaviours and style associated with the affective well-being of employees? A systematic review of three decades of research", *Work & Stress*, 24(2) (2010), pp. 107–39.

5. D. Montano, J.E. Schleu and J. Hüffmeier, "A meta-analysis of the relative contribution of leadership styles to followers' mental health", *Journal of Leadership & Organizational Studies*, 30(1), (2023), pp. 90–107.

6. D. Montano et al., "Leadership, followers' mental health and job performance in organizations: a comprehensive meta-analysis from an occupational health perspective," *Journal of Organizational Behavior*, 38(3) (2017), pp. 327–50.

7. V. Gang, "We asked 10 kids to 'draw a leader'. Here's what they did", *Fast Company* (May 22nd 2018).

8. D. Watson et al., "Well-being through learning: a systematic review of learning interventions in the workplace and their impact on well-being", *European Journal of Work and Organizational Psychology*, 27(2) (2018), pp. 247–68.

9. C. Tröster et al., "The coevolution of social networks and thoughts of quitting", *Academy of Management Journal*, 62(1) (2019), pp. 22–43.

Chapter 9: A wellbeing culture

1. J.E. Sheridan, "Organisational culture and employee retention", *Academy of Management Journal*, 35(5) (1992), pp. 1036–56.
2. G.G. Gordon and N. DiTomaso, "Predicting corporate performance from organisational culture", *Journal of Management Studies*, 29(6) (1992), pp. 783–98.
3. J.P. Kotter and J.L. Heskett, *Corporate Culture and Performance* (New York: Free Press, 1992).
4. J. Watts et al., "Evaluation of organisational culture and nurse burnout", *Nursing Management*, 20(6) (2013), pp. 24–9.
5. "Let's Talk", charlieclift.com
6. R.G. Booth et al., "Youth mental health services utilisation rates after a large-scale social media campaign: population-based interrupted time-series analysis", *JMIR Mental Health*, 5(2) (2018) e27.
7. N. Bloom, R. Han and J. Liang, "How hybrid working from home works out", NBER Working Paper w30292, National Bureau of Economic Research (July 27th 2022).
8. S. Subel, M. Stepanek and T. Roulet, "How shifts in remote behavior affect employee well-being", *MIT Sloan Management Review* (April 18th 2022).
9. Ibid.
10. See S.A. Ruhle et al., " 'To work, or not to work, that is the question'. Recent trends and avenues for research on presenteeism", *European Journal of Work and Organisational Psychology*, 29(3) (2020), pp. 344–63.
11. B. Laker et al., "Dear manager, you're holding too many meetings", *Harvard Business Review* (March 9th 2022).
12. A. Rimmer, "A third of ethnic minority staff working in mental health trusts have experienced harassment, bullying, or abuse at work", *British Medical Journal*, 374: n2220 (2021).
13. B. Sears et al., "LGBT people's experiences of workplace discrimination and harassment", William Institute UCLA School of Law (September 2021).
14. P. McDonald, "Workplace sexual harassment 30 years on: a review of the literature", *International Journal of Management Reviews*, 14(1) (2012), pp. 1–17.

15. R.S. Gold, L.J. Webb and J.K. Smith, "Racial differences in job satisfaction among white and black mental health employees", *Journal of Psychology*, 111(2) (1982), pp. 255–61.
16. S. Stenger and T.J. Roulet, "Pride against prejudice? The stakes of concealment and disclosure of a stigmatised identity for gay and lesbian auditors", *Work, Employment and Society*, 32(2) (2018), pp. 257–73.
17. J. Thornton, "Ethnic minority patients receive worse mental healthcare than white patients, review finds", *British Medical Journal*, 368:m1058 (2020).
18. Stenger and Roulet, "Pride against prejudice?"

Chapter 10: Wellbeing strategies, policies and support

1. The idea of a sieve model was initially designed for an article co-written with Benjamin Laker. See B. Laker and T. Roulet, "How organisations can promote employee wellness, now and post-pandemic", *MIT Sloan Management Review* (April 26th 2021).
2. Gartner's "2021 Employee Value Proposition Benchmarking Survey", cited in C. Valencia, "How to get employees to (actually) participate in well-being programs", *Harvard Business Review* (October 5th 2021).

Index

Page references for tables and diagrams appear in *italics*.